LOVE IS NEVER DONE

LOVE IS NEVER DONE

Reflections and resources for Holy Week

Neil Paynter

Contents of book © individual contributors
Compilation © 2021 Neil Paynter

First published 2021 by
Wild Goose Publications
Suite 9, Fairfield
1048 Govan Road, Glasgow G51 4XS, Scotland
the publishing division of the Iona Community.
Scottish Charity No. SC003794. Limited Company Reg. No. SC096243.

ISBN 978-1-84952-767-5

Cover photo: MacLean's Cross, Iona © David Coleman

All rights reserved. Apart from the circumstances described below relating to non-commercial use, no part of this publication may be reproduced in any form or by any means, including photocopying or any information storage or retrieval system, without written permission from the publisher via PLSclear.com.

Non-commercial use: The material in this book may be used non-commercially for worship and group work without written permission from the publisher. If photocopies of sections are made, please make full acknowledgement of the source, and report usage to CLA or other copyright organisation.

Neil Paynter has asserted his right in accordance with the Copyright, Designs and Patents Act, 1988, to be identified as the author of this compilation and the individual contributors have asserted their rights to be identified as authors of their contributions.

Overseas distribution
Australia: Willow Connection Pty Ltd, Unit 4A, 3–9 Kenneth Road, Manly Vale, NSW 2093
New Zealand: Pleroma, Higginson Street, Otane 4170, Central Hawkes Bay

Printed by Bell & Bain, Thornliebank, Glasgow

*To Alan Hawkins, 1942-2018,
friend and seeker of peace*

Contents

Introduction   9

REFLECTIONS

Palm Sunday, *With fresh eyes*, Ruth Harvey   15
Monday in Holy Week, *Turning the tables*, Martin Johnstone   21
Tuesday in Holy Week, *A lesson from the fig tree*, Jan Sutch Pickard   27
Wednesday in Holy Week, *Anointed with meaning*, Nancy Cocks   33
Maundy Thursday, *Before and after*, Craig Gardiner   37
Good Friday, *Seven last words*, Martin Wroe   43
Holy Saturday, *Buried*, Janet Lees   51
Easter Sunday, *Sunrise*, Brian Woodcock   55
Easter Monday, *A surprising encounter*, Peter Millar   61

RESOURCES

Palm Sunday
   Burdens, Tom Gordon   68
   Children of the stones, Warren R Bardsley   69
   God of crowds and God of crowns, the Corrymeela Community   70

Wednesday in Holy Week
   Anointing, Tom Gordon   72
   'Who touched me?', Peter Phillips   73
   In these strange times, Chris Polhill   75

Maundy Thursday
   Then Jesus took the towel, Carol Dixon   78
   The source of happiness, Murphy Davis   79
   God who washes our feet, the Corrymeela Community   82
   Love God and one another (even if they have smelly feet), Carol Dixon   82
   Break bread in new fields (A lockdown reflection), Judy Dinnen   83
   Sacrament, Tom Gordon   85
   One day, Judy Dinnen   86

Good Friday
   Praetorium, Sandra Sears   88
   Mediterranean Hope, Fiona Kendall   88

Remembering, Peter Millar   90
The cloak, Sandra Sears   91
Denial, Carol Dixon   92
Veronica's gift, Sandra Sears   93
Under the cross, Sandra Sears   94
He was held down (A prayer of confession), Carol Dixon   94
Crucifix, Sandra Sears   95
Breathe 2, Matt Sowerby   96
God of the crowds crying, 'Crucify!', the Corrymeela Community   97
The mother, Carol Dixon   97
Deposition, Anne Lawson   99
Here and now, Neil Paynter   100
Cross in the bus station, Warren R Bardsley   102
This is not the end: A reflection and meditation, Emma Major   103

Holy Saturday
Unravelling, Sandra Sears   108
Not just another Saturday, Tom Gordon   108
Suggestions for reflection and action on Holy Saturday, Ruth Burgess   110
A Saturday of waiting, Tom Gordon   111
Death cafés 2020, Ruth Burgess   112
God of grieving, the Corrymeela Community   113

Easter Sunday
A garden-grave, Janet Killeen   116
Fake news – a soldier speaks (Matthew 28:11–15), Carol Dixon   117
Daybreak, Janet Killeen   118
'Noli me tangere' (John 20:17), Carol Dixon   119
God of unbounded joy, the Corrymeela Community   119
A matter of where you're standing, Sandra Sears   120
The rising tide (Reflection on Easter Day 2020), Tom Gordon   122

On the road
The road to Emmaus, Jill Rhodes   124
Dear diary, Charlotte Killeya   126
Travelling, Janet Killeen   127
Two roads, John McCall   128
The other one, Brian Ford   130
Drift anchor (Reflection after Easter Day 2020), Tom Gordon   131

These are the feet, Peter Phillips   132
The road to Emmaus (A song), Stuart J Brock   134

Signs of hope
Introduction, Neil Paynter   136
The New Year's light, Israel Nelson   137
The hope that lies within me, Willie Salmond   137
Working for a more perfect day, Katharine M Preston   137
Growing hope for the future, Mark Reeve   138
The Poor People's Campaign (PPC), Leslie Withers   139
Million Moments for Democracy, Daniela and Tomas Bisek   139
So many people had helped him, Reinhild Traitler-Espiritu   140
Saidiana: A project of hope, Madge Irving   140
An encouraging story, Fridah Wafula and Marksen Masinde   141
The Tree of Life, June Walker   142
Light in the darkness, Frances Hawkey   143
Good news stories from around the world, David Hawkey   143
Hope is leading to action, Jean Belgrove   143
Steve can still laugh, Laura Gisbourne   144
Just to get a better view, Laura Murray   144
Something more, Rebekah Wilson   145
Hope (in two poems from Iona), Caro Penney   146
At Noor, Jill Rhodes   147
Birds over Nablus (2013), Warren R Bardsley   148
RSVP to a chain letter, Jan Sutch Pickard   149
I have a voice, Penny Walters   149
Signs of hope (to the reader)   151

Blessing, Thom M Shuman   154

About the contributors   155

Sources and acknowledgements   163

INTRODUCTION

Each year, when Holy Week and Easter rolls around, I remember some of the amazing people I met when I worked as a nurse's aide, and in homeless shelters.

I remember people like Andrew.

I met Andrew in a nursing home. Here's a little story I wrote about him:

'I'll make my pass on your starboard side,' Andrew calls out to me down the long narrow hallway. 'You know your starboard, don't ya? … Oh, you landlubbers,' he says with mock disgust, 'I tell ya! … I've just been doin' my exercises, you know.'

Andrew travels up and down the hallways of the home to stave off the stiffness of the rheumatoid arthritis creeping up his sinewy, tattooed arms. He is battling against the paralysis of his independence.

For there are many in the home, strapped into stilled silver wheelchairs. Each alone in his or her little boat. There is little current here. These are the horse latitudes of life: many in the home at the mercy of busy nurses in uniforms white as sails.

'I got to be gettin' back to my Jess,' Andrew says. 'The doctor was in again this week, you know. She's not doin' well.'

Andrew spends his days helping the nurses care for his wife – helping to change and clean and feed her. In his spare time, he talks into the tape recorder on his night table; or to Jessie, who doesn't answer any more; or to God and Jesus in the little stained-glass chapel, where he sometimes lights a candle.

Sometimes when I come, we sit out on the patio, and he tells me his stories:

About fighting in the First World War as a 'Jack tar', leaving from Scapa Flow when he was fifteen and a half. About fighting in Gallipoli. About another time, out in the foggy, cold Atlantic, arriving too late to save friends blown to bits by a U-boat; fishing for arms and legs, feeling sick with grief and the horror of war.

About his merchant marine days, and going on shore leave in Singapore. Strolling into a brothel there he didn't realise was a brothel ('I was only looking for a beer!') and suddenly getting caught up in a brawl – and getting tossed out a window; falling three stories into a cushioning heap of sewage and rubbish, and then having to go back to report to his commanding officer.

About driving a school bus for years, after immigrating to Canada.

About getting gangrene somehow and losing his legs. About coming home from the hospital.

Andrew and I talk; then sit in silence, watching the sunset. Occasionally, he puts some music on his phonograph, and dances. Balances, graceful as any dancer, on his bed, his shorts rolled up, free leg stubs swinging gaily to and fro to a recording of Scottish folk music.

I watched him dancing one day, and he was a vision of light to me.

Amazing – how someone can go through so much in their life and still dance. Lose their wife, lose friends, lose their legs, and still dance.

'Any regrets?' I asked him over the spirited music.

'I saw the world,' he said. 'And had a warm, wee house … I'm thankful,' he sang …

Whenever Holy Week rolls around, I remember people like Andrew, who remind me that *'the light shines in the darkness, and the darkness can never put it out'*; that *'love is never done'*.

Who do you remember during Holy Week? … Who are your witnesses to the Resurrection? …

Thank you to everyone who contributed to *Love Is Never Done*. I think of these books – with so many contributors – as little communities of hope. I hope that reading this book helps you to feel part of a community of hope. As 2021 dawns, we need hope.

Thank you to Sandra Kramer, Publishing Manager of Wild Goose, for her brilliance with layout and many other talents, and thanks too to Jane

Darroch Riley at Wild Goose. Thanks to both for their creativity, skill, support, humanness.

Thanks to member David Coleman for another beautiful cover photo: MacLean's Cross on Iona, which George MacLeod, in a classic old Iona Community pamphlet, describes as a 'Resurrection cross'. George writes:

> *'There are only three Resurrection crosses in Scotland. They show Christ on the Cross, not naked with a crown of thorns, but robed in splendour as a king: reigning from the Cross. The Divine Majesty is sufficiently revealed in the suffering humanity!*
>
> *In our day, humanity is coming into its own. Is it to kill itself, or to find … true stature in Christ?'*[1]

Neil Paynter, late winter, 2021

Note:

1. From *The Idea Whose Hour Is Come*, extracted in *Daily Readings with George MacLeod: Founder of the Iona Community*, Ron Ferguson (Ed.), Wild Goose Publications, republished 1991. (In this extract I've changed 'man' to 'humanity'.)

Reflections

Palm Sunday

Ruth Harvey

Bible reading:

When they were approaching Jerusalem, at Bethphage and Bethany, near the Mount of Olives, he sent two of his disciples and said to them, 'Go into the village ahead of you, and immediately as you enter it, you will find tied there a colt that has never been ridden; untie it and bring it. If anyone says to you, "Why are you doing this?" just say this, "The Lord needs it and will send it back here immediately."' They went away and found a colt tied near a door, outside in the street. As they were untying it, some of the bystanders said to them, 'What are you doing, untying the colt?' They told them what Jesus had said; and they allowed them to take it. Then they brought the colt to Jesus and threw their cloaks on it; and he sat on it. Many people spread their cloaks on the road, and others spread leafy branches that they had cut in the fields. Then those who went ahead and those who followed were shouting,

'Hosanna!
   Blessed is the one who comes in the name of the Lord!
   Blessed is the coming kingdom of our ancestor David!
Hosanna in the highest heaven!'

Then he entered Jerusalem and went into the temple; and when he had looked around at everything, as it was already late, he went out to Bethany with the twelve.

(Mark 11:1–11, NRSV)

Reflection: With fresh eyes

Two themes emerge for me as I read this Palm Sunday text. First, Jesus, as he enters Jerusalem, turns the world upside down. And then secondly, both in negotiating his transport, and entering through gates and crowds, we are introduced to the notion of a 'bystander'. What do these themes offer to you this Palm Sunday? In what ways do they help us approach Holy Week with fresh eyes?

Tapsalteerie

A king on a colt. Choosing to walk towards danger. The adulation of a crowd turning to condemnation. Has the world gone 'tapsalteerie'[1]?

These actions of Jesus as he approaches his final days signify not just a series of momentous events. They also signify a process, a methodology, a culture of *'turning the world upside down'* that was to be profoundly lasting. Echoing in action the words of Mary in the Magnificat (Luke 1:46–55), this man has come to turn our assumptions on their head. He will raise the poor and the hungry and bring the high and mighty down to earth. He will dispel the arrogance of the proud and propel the clarity of the humble. He will compel us to look at our assumptions and ask: do they serve those most in need?

In his entry into Jerusalem Jesus continues to turn the world tapsalteerie. Even his visit to the temple sets our heads reeling. Perceived wisdom, confirmed in other Gospels, is that Jesus angrily turned the tables in the temple. In Mark's version this act of turning the world of overconsumption upside down is itself turned on its head. Here the *'looking around'* that Jesus does in the temple, before turning and leaving, leaves us with a quiet question mark: what did Jesus see? *'Then he entered Jerusalem and went into the temple; and when he had looked around at everything, as it was already late, he went out' (Mark 11:11, NRSV).* What do we see when we look with fresh eyes on an upside-down world?

I remember as a child standing on my head, or holding my shins and looking through my legs at an upside-down world. I have a vivid experience growing up of lying on my back atop a much-loved hill on Iona, allowing my head to dangle over a safe ledge, giving me a tapsalteerie view of the world. Taking myself to a safe, high ledge to dangle upside down allowed me to notice the horizon in a new way as it danced with the colours and shades of sea and sky. This tapsalteerie vantage point still brings perspective, clarity and delight all at once. But I don't need to go to a specific hillside (and I'm out of practice at standing on my head!) in order to look out at the world with fresh eyes.

Bystander

Twelve of us travelled from Scotland in 2014 to Northern Ireland to meet with friends from the Corrymeela Community. We were a team of faith-based mediators seeking wisdom and guidance from these good friends about the nature of sectarianism and how we might respond. With the increase in sectarian violence, the Scottish Government had asked us to research the nature of religious sectarianism. The trouble with the Troubles, we were told, was that although the Good Friday Agreement of 10th April 1998 had largely brought peace, there was always the danger, the worry, the niggle that the embedded cultural norms that condoned condemnation of 'the other' because of their denominational belonging would rise to the surface once again, and 'trouble' the tender peace.

One evening we sat together at the Ballycastle Centre, which overlooks the north Atlantic, and watched a recorded series of groundbreaking interviews with those who had been impacted by the Troubles. First, we met the Bystanders[2] – those who had witnessed violence, abuse, prejudice, discrimination, even death – who had been terrified and terrorised. Their stories were sobering, transformative and startling, revealing the enormous impact of the Troubles on those who stood as witnesses. Many expressed their sense of impotence as violence unfolded in front of them, then their guilt, either because they had survived and their loved one had not, or because they had not stood up and spoken out in the face of discrimination or violence.

We are hard-wired to walk away from danger. Every instinct tells us to avoid violence, to protect ourselves and our loved ones. Standing by, watching, witnessing is a courageous act in itself. And yet always the question: what if I was to take a stand? The courage, the determination, the clarity and the foresight to take a stand, to walk towards potential danger is phenomenal.

Next, in a second series of interviews, we met a group called the Upstanders[3] who, in the face of all sensible advice, had chosen to take a stand or speak out against discrimination or violence. They had walked perilously towards danger, and slowly, little by little, helped through their changed behaviour to instil new habits which ultimately brought about a culture for good. One of the stories that stays with me is of a man who, at a football match, was uncomfortable with the sectarian songs being sung. Slowly, quietly, he began singing a different, inclusive song. Gradually, almost imperceptibly, the mood, and the song, around the stadium changed.

As Jesus moves towards danger and into Jerusalem, we are introduced to bystanders. We have no reason to doubt that these are, like us, good, reasonable people who lend the colt, open the gate, raise the palms, throw down their cloaks, welcome the procession, join in with the celebration. And yet we know that soon, very soon, some of these good people, so much like us, will become the ones enraged and goaded by a misguided leader to chant 'Crucify him.'

We enter Jerusalem, and we enter this Palm Sunday soberly accompanying Jesus as bystanders, hearing and watching him turn the world upside down. And asking always: how will we look out with fresh eyes on the world? What soft song might we sing to turn our bystanding head-over-heels, tapsalteerie, making upstanders of us all?

Prayer:

Loving God of our
tapsalteerie world
we pray for the agility
 of the toddler
and the daft-delight
 of the clown
that when we peer at the world
through our headstand gaze
we will see the world through your eyes.

 Then the lowly will be raised;
 the proud will fall;
 and we, bystanders, all
 together will find courage
  and compassion
 to step in and stand up
 to change the world for good.
Amen.

Actions:

- Consider the courage of the bystanders and the upstanders in the Corrymeela resources.

- Ask 'How might I look at the tapsalteerie world with fresh eyes?'

- Practise standing on your head or looking at an upside-down view.

Notes:

1. Scots for 'topsy-turvy' or upside down; pronounced 'tap-sul-tee-ree'.

2. *The Choices We Made: Bystanding and Conflict in Northern Ireland*: https://www.corrymeela.org/cmsfiles/resources/PeaceandConflict/TCWM-Ed-Guide-Final-for-WEB.pdf

3. 'UP Standing: Stories of Courage from Northern Ireland': https://www.corrymeela.org/news/28/up-standing-stories-of-courage

Monday in Holy Week

Martin Johnstone

Bible readings:

Matthew 21:12–17, John 12:7–8

Reflection: Turning the tables

Like many others, I grew up with a docile, mild and (to be honest) pathetic and anodyne caricature of Jesus. The Jesus who stood on the side of grown-ups and people in authority. It wasn't quite gentle Jesus, meek and mild but it wasn't far off it.

So it came as something of a surprise when I began to meet people who claimed to follow Jesus but burned with anger at injustice – people like Tricia, Alistair and John. They didn't fit with my experiences of Christianity or Church. Then I began to hear about martyrs in El Salvador, was introduced to the writings and life of Dietrich Bonhoeffer, and the prophetic, mischievous and marvellous joy of Desmond Tutu.

On Monday of Holy Week, we often read of Jesus' blazing anger as he entered the Temple, overturned the tables of the money lenders and raged against those who had made religion into a set of rules and an institution that profited on the backs of the poor.

He said to them, 'It is written,

"My house shall be called a house of prayer";
but you are making it a den of robbers.'

(Matthew 21:13, NRSV)

In Matthew, Mark and Luke this passage occurs directly after the triumphant entry into Jerusalem on Palm Sunday. In John's Gospel, it occurs earlier in Jesus' ministry. So, if we are reading John, the passage we tend to focus on relates instead to the anointing of Jesus' feet by Mary with extravagantly expensive nard (John 12:1–8). It includes Jesus' words: *'You always have the poor with you, but you do not always have me'* (John 12:8, NRSV).

This verse has often been used as a rationale for why we ought not to focus on the challenges of poverty and tackling injustice, focusing instead on private faith and adoration of a saccharine Jesus. But its meaning, I have come to realise, is exactly the opposite. We will always have the poor with us, not because that's what God wants but because of our failure to follow Jesus as we ought. Jesus' fury in the Temple courtyard was primarily focused on the religious authorities because they – we – ought to know better. With every fibre of our faith, we must resist our failure to live out the Gospel of light, love and justice.

Understanding change

A few years ago, I began to realise that the pursuit of justice happens at several different levels. I began to think of change as what we do, individually and collectively, with our head, heart, hands and feet.

- Think about the justice God calls us to pursue. What are the changes of policy that might enable justice to flow? (*Head*)

- Imagine a church and a society where those who are currently treated most unjustly are at the heart, not the margins, of our life together. What is the change of culture that might enable this to happen? (*Heart*)

- God is in the real and it is so often in the practical acts of service and love that the Gospel of justice comes to life. What are the things that we need to do to not just demonstrate God's anger at injustice but, in down-to-earth ways, show God's love for those too often treated without love. (*Hands*)

- Our pursuit of justice is shaped, in large measure, by who we journey with (or listen to). If we walk with those who exercise power, we are likely to remain unaware of the struggles of those who are marginalised every day. Who are the people that we will choose to spend our time with? (*Feet*)

A (not so) symbolic act

This reflection can be carried out individually or collectively (best in a small group):

- Read together an account of Jesus in the Temple (Matthew 21:12–17, Mark 11:15–19, Luke 19:45–48). Allow a period of silence to reflect upon the passage.

- Read together the story of Jesus' anointing at Bethany (John 12:1–8). Again, allow a period of silence to reflect upon the passage.

- Consider on your own (or together) a particular issue, or the experience of a person/community you know whose circumstances you believe leaves God angry. If you are doing this as a group, agree one issue to focus on.

- Consider your response with your head, heart, hands and feet. (If you are doing this as a group, you may want to have people write their proposed actions on four large sheets of paper, each with a symbol on them.)

  Head: What is the policy change that you are committed to bringing about?

  Heart: What is the change of culture you want to see happen?

  Hands: What is the practical thing that you are going to do?

  Feet: Who are you going to learn from?

Allow a decent amount of time as you move from head to heart to hands to feet – and do them in whatever order you wish. Then reflect prayerfully on what you will do.

Prayer:

God of anger,
enrage us.

Open our eyes to the things we do not see;
our ears to things we choose to ignore.

God of anger,
enrage us.

Open our minds to the possibilities of your community of love;
our hearts to the change you call us to be.

God of anger,
enrage us.

Open our hands to be generous with our gifts;
guide our feet to walk alongside the downtrodden.

God of anger,
enrage us,
and turn our rage
into love.

Amen.

Tuesday in Holy Week

Jan Sutch Pickard

Bible reading:

> ... now the winter is past,
>   the rain is over and gone.
> The flowers appear on the earth;
>   the time of singing has come,
> and the voice of the turtledove
>   is heard in our land.
> The fig tree puts forth its figs,
>   and the vines are in blossom;
>   they give forth fragrance.
>
> (Song of Songs 2:11–13, NRSV)

Reflection: A lesson from the fig tree

This is a beautiful time of year in the land that we call Holy: scarlet anemones, incense of wet earth after the rains, songs of mating birds, leaves of fig trees opening like little green hands. Living in a West Bank hill village, I enjoyed the blessings of creation described by the poet of the Song of Songs. Each spring, and now, the land will be transformed. Even on the edge of a bustling city like Jerusalem, spring is in the air. Jesus and his disciples would have seen and smelled and felt it as they walked over the hill from Bethany on their way to the Temple, in that last hectic week.

> On the following day, when they came from Bethany, he was hungry. Seeing in the distance a fig tree in leaf, he went to see whether perhaps he would find anything on it. When he came to it, he found nothing but leaves, for it was not the season for figs.
>
> (Mark 11:12–13, NRSV)

Growing up as a country boy, Jesus would have known well enough when the ripe purple figs would be ready to be plucked and eaten. Now there was only green fruit barely formed. But what did Jesus do?

> He said to it, 'May no one ever eat fruit from you again.' And his disciples heard it.
>
> (Mark 11:14, NRSV)

They had heard Jesus use fig trees as an example before:

> *'From the fig tree learn its lesson: as soon as its branch becomes tender and puts forth its leaves, you know that summer is near. So also, when you see these things taking place, you know that he is near, at the very gates ... Heaven and earth will pass away, but my words will not pass away.'*
>
> (Mark 13:28–29, 31, NRSV)

'Summer is near' – time ripening like fruit. Jesus pointed to the coming Kingdom of Heaven. But they were living in a time of watching and waiting. So why did Jesus curse the fig tree – which wasn't barren (in spite of the label that's often put on this story) but simply, slowly, fulfilling its promise?

- Was it the impetuous action of a hungry man living under stress?

- Was it as a sign that for Jesus, his followers and their mission, the time was running out?

- Or is this a story about deep disappointment – more than that, judgement – for promise unfulfilled?

What do you think?

That morning, the little group from out of town was heading for the Temple. All week, the great building in the heart of the city kept drawing them back. It had been a place of pilgrimage for their families and for many others over the centuries. *'A house of prayer for all nations.'* Yet what did they find when, among the day's pilgrims, they entered its gates?

They saw commerce, corruption in the Temple courts; no place for the poor, no welcome – only exploitation – for outsiders.

> *Then they came to Jerusalem. And he entered the temple and began to drive out those who were selling and those who were buying in the temple, and he overturned the tables of the money changers and the seats of those who sold doves; and he would not allow anyone to carry anything through the temple. He was teaching and saying, 'Is it not written, "My house shall be called a house of prayer for all the nations"? But you have made it a den of robbers.'*
>
> (Mark 11:15–17, NRSV)

As the story is told in Mark's Gospel, Jesus' words, and his dramatic action (tables overturned, merchants driven out, priests and politicians shocked), mirror the cursing of the fig tree.

All that promise, all that potential – in a tree, in a temple, in a place of powerful symbolism and secular power – but fruitless.

Fast forward two thousand years. The world is preoccupied by a pandemic. In one week two stories catch my eye – very different, but they both feel relevant. First, the nations – the world's peoples and their leaders – have been looking towards the Middle East. There is admiration and hope at the success of the State of Israel in running a mass vaccination programme, while other nations are still struggling. Green shoots of hope for all! But alongside this, there is growing concern at injustice.

Initially the Covid-19 vaccine rollout plan covered only citizens of Israel, including half a million Israeli settlers living inside the West Bank. It excluded the nearly five million Palestinians who live in the West Bank and Gaza Strip, under Israeli military occupation. Under international law an occupying power is responsible for the welfare of a people living under its control – including access to healthcare. While the Israeli Government was arguing that Palestinians had their own government which should be providing vaccines, that ignored the fact that politicians in the West Bank had much less agency and far fewer resources, while Gaza is effectively under siege.

I read about this in a January report from Amnesty International, and was angry. So much promise in health resources and skilled organisation, so much potential to benefit all the people in a small region of the world: but were these being shared fairly? Surely, in spite of the specious legal arguments, this was institutionalised discrimination – just as Jesus found in the Temple.

After several weeks of news coverage, and maybe as a response to criticism from around the world, the Israeli vaccination programme began to be extended to Palestinians in the Occupied Territories. My anger over this issue abated – but I'm well aware, from border restrictions, house demolitions, land confiscation, arbitrary imprisonments, of how far there is still to go, to bring justice to this troubled region.

So much promise, so much potential, like a flourishing fig tree. But where are the fruits? Where is the justice, in this or other places in the world, including our own country, where life-saving resources are not shared? What would Jesus do?

At the same time, I have been learning about the ways that places of worship have been used in the UK during the pandemic, when public worship was not possible: food banks, child care, storage of PPE, Covid-19 testing centres. Where would Jesus be in this 'secular' activity?

A picture lingers in my mind – of Salisbury Cathedral (among other spacious, airy, available 'holy places') this January, with many patient local people queuing, keeping their distance, while moving forward, hopefully, for their vaccinations.

A holy place still: resources shared, potential coming to fruit, a change of use (or policy) creating a place of healing.

Action: Find out more about the news stories mentioned here and what has happened (positive or negative) since.

Think of situations where justice still needs to be done, and where repentance – and change – is possible.

Prayer:

God of the world's goodness, greening and growth,
God of possibilities, of hope against hope,
help us to cope in the face of inhumanity –
not to condone others' pain, not become cynical, nor justify injustice.
Not to curse or condemn – but to watch, wait, work for change.
Help us to see the signs of your coming Kingdom,
when all may taste your goodness and find healing.
And, in the waiting time,
give us courage to believe in our common humanity
and to speak truth to power:
to light candles rather than to curse the darkness.
Amen.

Wednesday in Holy Week

Nancy Cocks

Bible reading:

While he was at Bethany in the house of Simon the leper, as he sat at the table, a woman came with an alabaster jar of very costly ointment of nard, and she broke open the jar and poured the ointment on his head.

(Mark 14:3, NRSV)

Reflection: Anointed with meaning (Mark 14:1–11)

It is just two days before Passover, Mark tells us, and the plot against Jesus is thickening. Yet the ominous mood set by the plotters (v. 1–2) is interrupted by a scene with beauty at its heart. As the aroma of the woman's perfume begins to fill the air, our senses are awakened to the tension in the room. It's tension created by symbols, words and actions, all resonant with layers of meaning. It's a moment preparing us for layers of meaning in what will happen on Friday – and on days and years to come.

The story opens with hospitality in the face of hostility. Hospitality can be such a beautiful thing, yet this meal is offered by Simon, a man made not so beautiful by a skin disease, something that names him unclean, perhaps disfigures him too. Some might turn down his invitation. But not Jesus. He is open to receive the gift of someone usually shut out of community.

In walks a woman, name unknown, to perform an intimate, tender gesture, so at odds with the public humiliation and cruelty looming on the horizon. It's an act of generosity, too, the alabaster jar broken, expensive perfume poured out lavishly. But the words used hint at deeper meanings. The Greek word for 'nard' sounds like the word 'myrrh', the burial perfume. The word 'pure' found in some translations contains 'faith' at its root. The act of anointing someone's head proclaims a royal identity, a divine purpose.[1] Meanings mix just like the scent of the perfume mixes in the air surrounding Jesus and the woman in this beautiful moment.

But the angry outburst from onlookers spoils the moment. This loving gesture seems too much. Too generous? Too beautiful? Ah, too wasteful! Yet even the word for 'waste' conveys a sense of the loss of a life 'wasted' in death.[2] The storyteller keeps weaving in subtle layers of meaning. As does Jesus when he commends the woman: *'She has done a good deed for me'*, he says, reminding listeners that scripture commends both anointing for burial and giving to the poor as good deeds. The words 'good deed' also suggest something 'beautiful'. Was it the beauty of her act that made Jesus' followers so anxious?

In Jesus' concluding words, this intimate, tender act becomes a parable of good news. *'Wherever the good news is proclaimed in the whole world, what she has done will be told in remembrance of her.'* The word for 'remembrance' referred to memorial stones in those days.[3] In these days, as we walk with Jesus towards his death, we also remember this woman, name lost to time but whose actions speak louder than those angry words. After all, Jesus points out that the woman has given all she has,[4] a subtle reminder that he too will give all he has – his life broken open and poured out on the Cross.

All these layers of meaning remind us that first impressions rarely tell us the whole story. How often have Jesus' words about the poor always being with us been twisted to imply that there is something more important than caring for those without enough? The final scene adds an ironic comment about this controversy. The plot to betray Jesus will turn on money, raising an eyebrow towards those who scolded the woman over the cost of her good deed. For truly, this story celebrates generosity – Simon's, offering hospitality in a dangerous time; the woman's, pouring out all she had to offer Jesus her love; both acknowledging and anticipating Jesus' generosity. And soon we will see his generous act on the Cross. This story calls us to consider not only his generosity, but our own.

Layer upon layer of meaning keeps anointing our contemplation of this story, just like the lingering scent of perfume reminds us of the presence of someone who has already left the room. There is not just one meaning, one definitive interpretation of this story Mark has placed so close to the final drama in Jesus' life. For Jesus' giving of himself has more than one meaning, too, depending on our situation, our needs and our hopes. When we face danger, when tragedy and loss have scored against us, when it seems those we trusted have betrayed or abandoned us, Jesus is with us, friend to the end. The Cross proclaims this truth from its heart. But when we have done something wrong, something that makes us ashamed, something we cannot fix ourselves, Jesus lifts these burdens from us with the arms of the Cross, his mercy unending. And when we pour ourselves out in generosity, Jesus remembers us too. The good news of God's generosity is proclaimed again and again when we find ways to anoint the world in Jesus' name. For in a profound sense, the Cross is not the final drama in Jesus' life. His life is lived out in us, again and again, in good deeds and beautiful actions which continue to tell the story of God's generous love, poured out for us – and poured out through us.

Prayer:

Jesus,
friend to the end,
stay with us when life is unrelenting;
walk with us when terror or tragedy surrounds us.

Jesus,
mercy unending,
pour your grace over us
when shame and regret burn within;
anoint us with forgiveness to help us make amends.

By your generosity,
inspire us to pour ourselves out
in compassion for the poor of the earth,
to make justice in your name.

With your compassion,
accompany us in honoring those who have died
and comforting those who mourn.
We offer what is good and beautiful in our lives
to anoint the world with your undying love.
Amen.

Note:

1-4. The study of meanings in the Greek is based on Joel Marcus' commentary, 'Mark 8-16', Vol 27A in the Anchor Yale Bible Series © 2009 Yale University

Maundy Thursday

Craig Gardiner

Bible reading:

John 13

Reflection: Before and after

Maundy Thursday brings us to the supper Jesus shared with his friends in the Upper Room.

But there is a before and an after to this meal of remembrance. That also ought to be recalled.

Eating together was important to Jesus. At weddings with family, at picnics with strangers, meals were often eaten, in strange places, at unlawful times and with forbidden people: It's what often got him into trouble.

But it was not so much the menu as the guests he deemed important. People mattered, especially those who didn't matter at any other table.

It is no surprise, then, that before his death, they had a meal together, a 'last supper' between friends.

Many more were there perhaps than da Vinci's tidy artistry would have us believe: there would be women and children too. It's difficult to read the gospels and think otherwise.

Each follower was affirming their relationship with one another and with God: around a ritual feast multilayered with memories of liberation, forming a fulcrum of new belonging in the body of Christ.

On this day it is right and proper that we participate again, with thanks and joy in the breaking of bread and the sharing of wine.

Recalling his words: *'Take and eat; this is my body given for you. Drink, for this cup is the new covenant in my blood. Do this to remember me and what we do in this upper room.'*

But we ought not to rush to the table. Nor linger there too long.

There is a before and an after to this meal that warrants our devotion too.

If we are to truly be the body of Christ, there is a before.

Maundy Thursday 39

Before the bread and before the wine, John's Gospel takes seriously the physical imagery. The body of Christ cannot be reduced to some spiritual metaphor. Because, as the meal is shared, the disciples watch wide-eyed, slack-jawed as Jesus wraps a towel round his waist and faces his body towards theirs.

He dips his hands. Immerses his fingers in the unacknowledged sacrament. Then holds the feet, touches the toes, blesses the arch, the heal, the body of each disciple, and commands them, and us, to love one another, the body of Christ.

Hold one another, wash one another in intimate, vulnerable service.

Love these bodies, bear their burdens, hear their fears, trust their intentions, even the ones who are not like us and those we suspect may yet betray us, or those we know we have already betrayed.

All this happens before they had eaten.

So we ought not rush to the table. Scurrying past the basin, the towel, the bodies and the command like some inconvenient overture.

Not before we have knowingly obeyed and practised what we preach of love. For only those who obey have truly believed, fully belonged and really known love.

And this is how the world will know Christ's disciples: that we love one another.

So, let us find joy in the bread and the wine, communion with God, community with one another.

But let us not rush too quickly home: For there is an after just as there was a before.

This after takes us to the garden, picking our way through the night-light past half-hidden tree roots and creeping shadows.

Where Jesus engages the deepest temptations to wrestle with doubt and fear, to grapple with God, seeking out Gethsemane to reclaim our Eden.

After the eating and the drinking, the body that washes the bodies of others is at his most human ... most like our own living, even as he struggles to fulfil God's purpose.

And yet we rarely journey here, and if we do, we fear to linger in the garden after the table and seldom dare to be disturbed by this recapitulation of the Fall.

Is it any wonder when we consider what is entrusted to us?

As the Community of Taizé sing the challenge:

> *Stay with me,*
> *remain here with me,*
> *watch and pray ...*[1]

Here is the mystery of the Incarnation: Jesus, fully God ... and yet fully human: vulnerable, suffering and seeking our help.

That's not what we expect from God.

We often believe that God is there to offer help to us: to bring us healing, freedom, salvation.

What are we to do with a God who needs our help? Who asks us to wait and watch and pray.

Religion offers many ways to invoke God to act on our behalf, to uncover a transaction that assures us; if you do this, then God will do the other.

But, as George MacLeod would say, *'Jesus doesn't come to bring us more religion. He comes to abolish it.'*

That may not be what is expected. But it's what we discover in the garden ... if we wait there long enough.

It is also what Dietrich Bonhoeffer discovered. Not in a garden but in a Nazi prison cell. His Gethsemane from which he wrote the poem 'Christians and others'.[2]

In the poem he says many folk go to God when they need rescuing from their troubles, expecting God to save them; but then he turns that image on its head, asking what might happen when God is in need of our help, when the Christ who is found in anyone of us is hungry, homeless or suffering in some other way.

His answer is that we, as Christians, should stand in solidarity with God amidst the divine suffering, doing all we can to bring healing and relief.

The truth of this evening is that we must learn to stand by God in Christ's time of suffering. And surely Christ suffers most: when the least of creation, its people, its planet is reviled, rejected, abused and ignored.

Bonhoeffer knew enough personal anguish for us to take him seriously. He'd watched and prayed with others in their Gethsemane, and dared to hope that they might stand by him in his.

Christ saves us, not by being all-powerful, but as he has shown us all along, in his weaknesses, for only a suffering God can help.

This is what we learn in the garden. This is what comes after the table.

We are dismissed into the pain of Good Friday, the bewilderment of Saturday and summoned again to take up our cross to participate in God's distress at the hands of the world.

This is what makes a Christian faithful. Our identification with God's suffering in the world. Our waiting, our watching, our praying for the crucified people of today.

But where do we find the grace to live like this?

The final verse of Bonhoeffer's poem offers some hopeful direction and a glimpse, perhaps, of resurrection too. As we leave the table, we remember what has gone before and what will indeed come after: God will come to everyone, Christian or otherwise, and on the Easter cross and from the empty tomb, Christ forgives us all.

Notes:

1. 'Stay with me' © Ateliers et Presses de Taizé, 71250 Taizé, France

2. See 'Christians and heathens', from *Letters and Papers from Prison*, Dietrich Bonhoeffer, Fortress Press, 2005, p.461. (This title is variously translated as 'Christians and heathens/pagans/others'.)

Good Friday

Martin Wroe

Seven last words

FORGIVE

> When they came to the place that is called The Skull, they crucified Jesus there with the criminals, one on his right and one on his left. Then Jesus said, 'Father, forgive them; for they do not know what they are doing.'
>
> (Luke 23:33–34a, NRSV)

Maybe the two criminals, caught red-handed on their last job, had fallen out with each other. Perhaps the only way to shut them up was to put the quiet guy in between.

'Forgive them,' says Jesus, as the nails bite. 'Forgive them. They don't know what's going on.'

Of all the low-life rogues to find the long arm of the law landing on their shoulders, these two get to hang right in the middle of history. Unlike Mary or Peter or Judas, they'd never lived with Jesus. Instead they get to die with him. No chance to give him their lives. Only their deaths.

Soldiers, thieves, rubbernecking spectators. Intrigued or wincing or averting our eyes. Wishing this had not been our shift, hoping nothing's about to kick off. No one in this first Easter scene knows quite what's going on. Not quite sure how we ended up here. Not knowing we could ask for forgiveness. Not knowing someone else has.

REMEMBER

> Then he said, 'Jesus, remember me when you come into your kingdom.' He replied, 'Truly I tell you, today you will be with me in Paradise.'
>
> (Luke 23:42–43, NRSV)

Hanging, they used to say, concentrates the mind. This is one concentrated mind. Life zoomed into sharp focus. Everything worth seeing in sharp hi-def.

Something understood.

Something that tells this man not to join the soldiers in humiliating his broken brother on the cross. Tortured to the end of himself but still with some mysterious strength. Weakness a kind of power.

On the brink of being forgotten, we understand how good it would be to be remembered. And something in this broken brother seems to say that if he remembered you, then you would never be forgotten again.

You will be with me today in a place where the dead are living. Where love has won. Where justice rolls down like a river and all these days we call life are seen through some other lens.

'You will be with me today,' says Jesus. As if he understands something.

We remember someone as though we might give them extra life.

Jesus remembers us and we are never forgotten again.

OTHERS

> *When Jesus saw his mother and the disciple whom he loved standing beside her, he said to his mother, 'Woman, here is your son.' Then he said to the disciple, 'Here is your mother.' And from that hour the disciple took her into his own home.*
>
> (John 19:26–27, NRSV)

What does a mother think as she watches her son dying, slowly, by degrees. I wish it had never come to this? I wish I'd never had him?

And what about the favourite follower? So much for being in the inner circle, when the circle is being bent and broken before you. When all your hopes and dreams are being drained of life in front of your eyes.

Or the squaddies, dicing for a dying man's clothes, not knowing they have ringside seats at a cosmic drama?

And in the mind of the event-seekers? Those whose curiosity slowed them to a halt at the sight of these bodies silhouetted high against the sky. Wait till I get home and tell everyone about this.

Which of us knows what any of us are thinking? We can barely read our own minds. Which of us knows the part we are playing in the story being written before us?

We only know for sure what Jesus was thinking of.

He was thinking of others.

As usual.

GODFORSAKEN

> At three o'clock Jesus cried out with a loud voice, 'Eloi, Eloi, lema sabachthani?' which means, 'My God, my God, why have you forsaken me?'
>
> (Mark 15:34, NRSV)

Is there a time and place when even the immortal invisible has had enough of us?

Is this God hiding from Jesus? Or has Jesus lost sight of God? When it comes down to it, what's the difference?

If we believe that Jesus, somehow, was also God, then here is God taking leave of God.

A divine defeat.

As darkness falls, confusion rises.

Voices drop away, disappear.

Spectators wander off.

Now only the silent sound of hope as it is forsaken.

One more life, abandoned to fate in the middle of history.

You have to lose your life in order to find it.

Jesus used to say that.

THIRST

After this, when Jesus knew that all was now finished, he said (in order to fulfil the scripture), 'I am thirsty.'

(John 19:28, NRSV)

Everybody is dying for a drink. We live on a blue planet holding 326 million cubic miles of water, each of those a gigantic cup holding more than a trillion gallons.

Our bodies are mainly made of water and without it we shrivel up and cease to be. Our life runs dry.

But water alone does not bring us life.

Each of us is thirsty for something else. An infusion to transcend the physical, to sustain us deep inside.

'Let anyone who is thirsty come to me,' he had said. But now this great spring of life is running drying.

Thirstier than he has ever been. Because we are all dying of thirst.

ANGER

Then Jesus, crying with a loud voice, said, 'Father, into your hands I commend my spirit.' Having said this, he breathed his last.

(Luke 23:46, NRSV)

He's not beaten, even when he's defeated.

Desperate and dying.

Abandoned.

But still, with his final breath, angry at the gulf between the way things are and the way things might be.

Shouting at the invisible.

What can you do but shout when you see the distance between the way things are and the way things might be?

Howling your prayers.

Yelling your psalms.

If you can't shout at God, who can you shout at?

And if you think the decibels can climb across the unknown, can be heard by Love and that Love will answer ... then you jump.

Trusting only the unseen hands of mercy, the hands that always made everything from nothing. Always will.

What other hands dare we fall into?

Perhaps we are not abandoned.

Perhaps we are not beaten. Even when we are defeated.

EVERYTHING

> *When Jesus had received the wine, he said, 'It is finished.' Then he bowed his head and gave up his spirit.*
>
> (John 19:30, NRSV)

Clear the area please. Nothing left to see. Jesus has left the building. Has left us all.

In the beginning was the Word and the Word is now sentenced. Full stop. Close quotes. New paragraph.

Whatever 'everything' is, 'everything' is now complete.

Things seen. Things unseen. Things in between.

Everything that was started has finished.

Every beginning has found its loose end, all thoughts taken to their logical conclusion.

On this day, we have seen it all.

Everything dies.
Life dies.
Death dies.
Everything is done.

Except love.

Only love is not done.
Only love will not die.
Everything is finished except love.

Love bears all things,
believes all things,
hopes all things,
endures all things.

At some point everything will be done.
Except love.
Love is never done.

Holy Saturday

Janet Lees

Bible reading:

He was buried.

From my remembered Bible

Reflection: Buried

When I was a school chaplain, I was asked by one family if I would conduct the funeral of the great-grandmother of two of the pupils. It was the elder, aged 14, who had suggested it and I was ready to respond. The younger, a boy of six years old, had a lot of questions about getting great-grandma buried.

It was to be a graveside service and as we walked into the very large municipal cemetery to a plot some distance away, a small hand found its way into mine and we walked along together. As we arrived at the grave, green cloths covered the earth that had been taken out and piled alongside. Great-grandad had been buried in the same grave some years previously. This had been at the root of most of the questions from my companion. Although he'd not known his great-grandfather, he was curious about this burying business: 'What would we see in the grave?'

So we'd talked about that, and as we came to the lip of the grave, each holding the hand of the other, we looked down, and sure enough there was another coffin already there: great-grandad waiting for great-grandma to join him. As the service progressed my companion kept tight hold of my hand; and when the time came to put some earth in the grave, he joined in with everyone else and together we buried great-grandma ...

Are you, too, curious about this burying business?

Have you seen the piles of earth, the sea of floral tributes as the past year progressed?

Wondered about those who have buried loved ones with little opportunity to mourn?

Been concerned for the professional buriers with the stress and pressure of the last year?

Prayer:

You who have seen loved ones buried,
in explosion or flood,
on ocean floor or through mountain landslip,
whatever the tomb, God knows the place,
and like a persistent sniffer dog,
searches us out, marks our lives, says,
'There's another one over here.'

(You may want to name, in silence or aloud, or mark in another way, the names of those buried, or the places of those burials ...)

God of the empty space, as we balance on the edge,
may we know you as the Edge-wise One,
who saw your own Son buried.

There has been a lot of burying:

Buried, the truth consigned to the dark.

Buried, the elderly isolated from family in care homes

Buried, young people facing challenges to their mental health,
with little support.

Buried under a mound of misused statistics and an avalanche of lies.

Buried by a cascade of confusion, dug under by denial,
lost and lamented, a generation culled.

The exhausted and anxious have worked on,
that the ventilated might still breathe
and the dead be buried with dignity.

There is no one who deserves to be buried:
a cull based on age or infirmity is not based on 'kindom' values.
A virus may run unhindered in places of poverty,
but we are called to protect the poor and vulnerable.

(You may want to name the protectors, those who have offered help and support, who have been there alongside ...)

When the day comes,
after this ghastly descent,
when the dead rise, though changed,
and we meet in the clear air,
we will see each other face to face again.

Any of us could have been buried,
or buried those close to us.
Only One, having descended so far,
can rise again and take us on a new adventure:

Hell-confronter, hold our fears.
Stone-roller, release us.
Tomb-quitter, raise us up!

Action:

If you can find some soil or a clod of earth, touch it; pick it up if you can and weigh it in your hands. Get the earth on your fingers, under your fingernails if possible. If you have companions with you, pass the earth to them that they might do the same.

Crumble the soil back onto the ground. Look at your dirty hands. Turn them face upwards; admire them.

Of course you will probably wash this off, but you can do it again, almost any time, to remind you: *From earth we come, to earth we return.*

Easter Sunday

Brian Woodcock

Bible readings:

> ... very early on the first day of the week, when the sun had risen, they went to the tomb.
>
> (Mark 16:2, NRSV)

> ... as yet they did not understand ...
>
> (John 20:9, NRSV)

Reflection: Sunrise

I'm writing this as I emerge from Epiphany 2021.
So, to me, it doesn't feel very much like Easter.
The magi have just departed by another route,
leaving Mary and Joseph to take their child
and flee for their lives; for *his* life.
They are yet to see him growing up,
or to watch with alarm as, at the age of thirty,
he gathers a group of bewildered disciples
and embarks on his reckless ministry
that enchants the populace and enrages the authorities ...
until the bubble bursts.

It's a journey we, too, are invited to take,
sharing in the highs and lows of it all
till it reaches this day of rejoicing.

But how am I to rejoice at the climax
when, for me, the story has hardly started?
As I write this, it doesn't feel like Easter.

There's another reason it doesn't feel like Easter, as well.
As I write we've gone into lockdown again.
Whatever will be happening this Easter
(and the signs aren't good from where I am just now)
I can't forget the last one, when churches were closed;
and we couldn't gather to sing our praises out loud,
or shout 'He is risen indeed!'

But, of course,
it didn't feel like Easter then, either –
the first time, when it all happened
(whatever it actually was that happened).
Danger in the air.
Disciples in hiding, with doors locked and bolted.
A small group of women, carrying burial spices,
creeping through empty streets, hoping not to meet anyone.
Very early. Still dark.

They had been shrouded in darkness
since the morning of the great darkness, two days back.
They weren't ready to see the rising of the sun.
They had a job to do. It had been delayed.
Nothing else mattered just now.
Oh, one thing mattered: how to move that huge stone!

But when they reached the garden, what was this?
Oh God!
The tomb already open! The body missing!
A strange man in white, saying strange things.
Seized with terror, they ran.

That's where the story gets confusing,
if it wasn't confusing enough already.
According to Mark, they said nothing to anyone.
Luke reckons they told the disciples but weren't believed.
As for John's account, there was some coming and going,
with Mary Magdalene ending up alone by the tomb,
weeping, encountering more strangers,
and demanding that the gardener tell her where he has put the body.

And then:
'Mary!'
The moment of recognition!
The first to see the risen Son!
The first also to experience the pain of social distancing.
'Do not hold me ... I am going to the Father.'
The first to realise things could never go back
and be the same as before.

Later that day, the disciples in lockdown:
'Peace be with you.'
Days later, two of them walking to a nearby village,
so clouded by grief they couldn't see who had come alongside them,
engaging them in conversation.
Still later, some of them returning to their old occupation
of fishing for fish, for want of anything better to do,
and seeming to have lost their touch
till the stranger on the shore came to their aid.

Every time, they were surprised;
and every time, overjoyed.
'The Lord is risen! He is risen indeed!' –
but always surprised.
It took a while for the light to dawn,
the light of sunrise; the light at the end of the tunnel.
Only little by little were they able to take it in –
that it had really happened.
Not just for him. For them.
For all his people.
They would all be living his risen life now!

Instant change might have been a flash in the pan.
Transformation evolves.
They had to wait for the light to dawn.

And the dawning came:
hiding ones stepped into the open,
and frightened ones spoke out;
those who had withdrawn into their shells or their past
embraced an unknown future;
mourning turned into dancing, weeping to joy,
as the sun, that had always been there,
broke though.

'Because I live, you, too, will live!' he said.
We live because he lives!

Prayer – a cry for help

'Why do you look for the living among the dead?
He is risen,' they said. 'He is not here.'

No, but I am!

Come, risen Lord, you who promised to be with us always,
to the end of time; to the ends of the earth.
Come and find me.
Lead me out of this tomb –
out to a place of hope and healing;
where the news is good and truth sets us free
and the whole world is full of possibility;
where change can happen, and will,
and streets fill with laughter, and banners proclaim:
'This is the first day of the rest of your life.'

Easter Monday

Peter Millar

Bible reading:

Luke 24:13–35

> Now on that same day two of them were going to a village called Emmaus, about seven miles from Jerusalem, and talking with each other about all these things that had happened. While they were talking and discussing, Jesus himself came near and went with them ...

(Lk 24:13–15)

Reflection: A surprising encounter

Over the years, it has been my privilege to reflect on this famous passage in Luke's Gospel, not just in my native Scotland but also in India, Australia, the States and South Africa. In the discussions that followed my talk many people shared their own experience of meeting Christ in surprising ways. These encounters have been life-changing and are a marker of Christian experience through the centuries. People from every culture on this earth feel that their very name has been called by the One who walks with them.

In this text, Luke invites us into that experience which is seminal in Christianity. That is, the realisation that belief in Jesus is not the understanding of a philosophy, but the meeting of an individual with a person who can bring to one's life an inner transformation. Within this text there are many things which biblical scholars have argued about for centuries, but it is important for us to see beyond the seeming contradictions in the words, to the wider picture. And that larger picture contains life-giving truths which have a powerful relevance for our often complicated and uncertain lives in a world which today carries unchartered markers of turbulence.

A basic question for us all is – do we allow this Jesus to walk with us day by day? God's invitation is always tender. Those on the road to Emmaus all these years ago initially had no clue that Jesus was close to them. Yet as Cleopas and his companion ate with Jesus in the evening of that day, they recognised him, and, as the gospel says, *'their hearts burnt within them'*. Two thousand years later, we do not need to know every single detail of that meeting. What is important is that dawning recognition – that inner journey of spiritual awakening within these two individuals. They were on that pathway which is inherent in all the great religions of the world – the journey from darkness into light. I see it as the 'reconnecting' with our true selves – becoming aware that deep within us we carry the image of God. That we are held in love no matter how tough the journey.

In one of his great poems, the Welsh poet R.S. Thomas speaks of Christ *'listening'* to our prayers through all of time. In that listening our heartbeat meets the heartbeat of God. Yet how that happens is always a mystery in the sense that it is not something we can closely define. That is why every single spiritual journey has its own particular characteristics. No two humans are exactly alike and in the same way our encounters with the divine are all different. As the friends walked toward Emmaus they were walking unknowingly into the Light. They were embracing the Mystery. And to discover the Mystery is to embrace the real. To glimpse the morning star.

Sometimes it is no more than a flicker of light through the cloud of unknowing, as many great writers and poets remind us. Yet as we begin to look more closely, and often from the darkness that surrounds us, we meet with the One who actually walks with us all the time, and who illumines our faces and meets the longings of our soul. Yet more than that – this is the One who, day by day, guides us to that *'path of compassion'* where truth, justice and ultimate hope infuse all reality and give meaning to our endeavours.

And at the very heart of this encounter is the element of surprise – as it was on the Emmaus road. Christianity without this element is somehow incomplete. We don't know that moment or the time when we shall know deep within us that we have encountered Light and been awakened to the energies of God. That moment when it becomes clear to us that we have been befriended by Christ and empowered by God's ever-moving Spirit which will take us far beyond where we ever thought we would go in terms of our soul.

Many years ago I tried to say something about all of this in a prayer. When I wrote it, I never imagined a global pandemic or the rise of dictators around the world; I had not fully understood the enormity of climate change nor the fact that in the years ahead millions of my sisters and brothers would be experiencing new and terrible levels of poverty. I had never heard of Me Too or Black Lives Matter; I had not experienced, as I have now, what it meant to live with an incurable cancer. Yet what I wrote back then is still relevant and I hope its words will give us renewed courage to walk closely with Christ on today's uncertain paths.

Prayer:

Don't hide, don't run
but rather discover
in the midst of fragmentation
a new way forward,
a different kind of journey
marked by its fragility and lack of definition.

And on that path
to hold these hands that
even in their brokenness
create a new tomorrow.

To dance at the margins
and to see the face of Christ
where hurt is real and pain a way of life.

To be touched in the eye of the storm,
aware that tomorrow may not bring peace.

'Impossible,' you say.
'Let me retreat and find my rest.'

What rest, my friend,
in these fragmented times?

Resources

Palm Sunday

Burdens

Bear one another's burdens, and in this way you will fulfil the law of Christ.

(Galatians 6:2, NRSV)

Palm Sunday begins with a strange journey, with Jesus – in a local parody of a Roman Triumph – coming into Jerusalem riding on a donkey.

Because of the restrictions on us at present, many will struggle with not being in our churches to celebrate and re-enact this amazing scene. We can't sing our 'Hosannas'; march around the church or our community; wave our branches; distribute our palm crosses. So, I suggest you close your eyes for a moment today, and take yourself back to a Palm Sunday event that's been important to you: think of the songs; feel the excitement; picture the smiling faces – and you will be there to celebrate.

But might I also suggest something else? Take a moment to spare a thought for the donkey. No donkey: no means of transport for Jesus; no donkey: no re-enactment of a Triumph; no donkey: no Palm Sunday story. A 'beast of burden' had done what needed to be done. That's all. It carried its passenger, and made it all happen.

There are many people carrying burdens for us today, particularly our Health Service staff, called on when needed, caring for us, carrying us, doing what needs to be done.

Prayer:

Thank you, God, for the people who carry my burdens today. And if I'm called on to carry someone else's, give me strength for the journey, and give me humility to keep doing what needs to be done. Amen.

Tom Gordon

Children of the stones

Inspired by an article in the Israeli newspaper Haaretz, *about a ten-year-old boy shot dead by Israeli soldiers as he threw a stone at their tank (2012).*

Throwing stones.
Well, it's a thing children do, isn't it?
Not normally to be condoned,
but – if that is what defines you,
what then?
What else can you do
when faced by tear gas,
bombs and bullets?

We salute you Mustapha
and all children of the stones.
We salute your brave
resistance in the face
of relentless tyranny.

What else could you do?

If we who do not throw stones
remain silent as injustice rules and
oppression stalks the land,
will the stones themselves
cry out?

Warren R Bardsley

God of crowds and God of crowns

God of crowds and God of crowns:
in your humility,
on the back of a donkey,
at the start of a week of great pain,
you showed a determination
to save us
not with overwhelming force
but with self-giving, revolutionary love.
May we see in your life and death,
and in your resurrection,
the way to face the foes within.
May we overcome our fears,
and put down our selfish wants;
may we stop our tendency to blame,
and fight for others first.
As you shield us from what we can't control,
save us from ourselves.
Amen.

Corrymeela Community

Wednesday in Holy Week

Anointing

Thou hast anointed my head with oil; my cup runneth over.

(Psalm 23:5, KJV)

The Presbyterian tradition of the Christian Church doesn't give itself much to anointing. But I was deeply moved in my time as a hospice chaplain by a story from an Anglican chaplain who was often called on as part of her ministry to anoint patients with holy oil in their last days.

There had been a death in her hospice which had affected everyone deeply. The nurses doing the 'last offices' asked for her to come to anoint the body as a final act of love and care. She rushed into the room to 'do the necessary', only to find that she'd forgotten the Holy Oil. The nurses were in tears, and the chaplain was soon in tears too. So she did what needed to be done – she took the tears from the cheek of one of the nurses and used that to anoint the patient. A 'proper' anointing? You bet it was, for everyone in that room was anointed with holiness and love in their own way.

Years later, on a pilgrimage to the Holy Land, our party stopped by the River Jordan. Our Muslim coach-driver filled a bottle with water from the river, came over to me, and poured the water over my outstretched hands. In a moment of holiness and healing, I was anointed too.

On this day of Holy Week, we remember a woman using expensive oil to anoint Jesus at Bethany. In an offering of unconditional love, a holy moment was created. If today, you anoint someone with your tears, or offer healing in an act of compassion, or give love unconditionally, you are creating something profoundly holy for them and for you, and a cup of blessing for them and for you will, once again, brim to overflowing.

Prayer:

Anoint me with your love today, Holy God, that I might in compassion offer the sacrament of your blessing to those around me. Amen.

Tom Gordon

'Who touched me?'

Introduction, by Peter Phillips:

Due to being diagnosed with motor neuron disease in April 2019, my health has deteriorated considerably, but what has been more remarkable, my life has completely changed ... for the better.

As well as being able to reconnect with old friends, the 'new' people I have met and worshipped among have been a real blessing. But, my gift didn't stop there ... No.

I began to compose a collection of 'poetry' about all sorts of things, for the first time in my life. Friends were surprised that some of my poems spoke to them on a very deep and spiritual level ... and this is why I truly believe my motor neuron disease is a 'gift from God'.

I believe that, through each one of us, God is working and calling us to 'get out there' and to proclaim His Kingdom here on earth.

When we come across wrongdoing, injustice and human suffering, such as climate change, poverty, 70 million refugees, Christians must not be afraid to speak out and act. Having a terminal illness has not changed that. For me, it will remain a gift, and I pray others will discover the gifts of their own mortality one day too. After all: to live in Christ, and to die ... would be a real gain. Don't you think? ...

'Who touched me?'
I did, Lord, I touched you.
In a moment of desperation ...
... I touched you.
It has taken me a lifetime ...
to get close to you.
It has taken all my courage ...
... to come this close to you.
I have been hesitant;
I have felt downtrodden by my own
unworthiness and guilt.
Unable to approach you,
I have stood on the brink of a precipice ...

... but, I was too much of a coward ...
... to step off into the unknown.
So, I crawled back.
Back to my life of fear ...
... resentment and selfishness.

Yes, I touched you, Lord Jesus.
I touched you, when I was in isolation.

I touched you, when I was ...
... holding the hand of a dying companion.

I touched you in a prison cell.

I touched you as I waited for essential food ...
... at the foodbank.

I touched you in ...
... the mist of terminal illness.

I touched you, Lord, as ...
... I watched Alan Kurdi drown in front of me.
I touched you, Jesus, as a nameless child ...
... died of starvation in the Yemen.

Jesus, simply by touching you ...
the whole world becomes aware of your healing grace.
Thy will be done on earth, as it is in Heaven.

Peter Phillips, August 2020

In these strange times

Living God,
in these strange times
where touch is denied
and smiles are hidden,
may we know your touch
on our lives.

May your healing and peace
renew us,
body, mind and spirit,
keeping a deep smile in our hearts.

Chris Polhill, Iona Prayer Circle Coordinator, 2020

Iona Prayer Circle:
https://iona.org.uk/about-us/prayer/the-iona-prayer-circle
prayercircle@iona.org.uk

Maundy Thursday

Then Jesus took the towel

It was Mary who started it –
who sowed the seed of the idea
in my mind to wash the feet of my friends.
Her absolute humility, and adoration,
as she poured out the perfumed ointment,
anointing me for my burial.
She didn't care that others
were scandalised, as Peter was
when I first knelt to wash his feet,
yet in the end he embraced the act with joy.

I'll never know what Judas felt;
perhaps he was revolted as I stooped
before him, offering my wholehearted love.
Something had changed in him
the night he saw Mary prostrate herself at my feet;
the crisis had been coming for a while.

It wasn't just the money, it was her utter devotion;
maybe he suspected he could never match that,
and second best was not enough for him.
So he distanced himself from me,
from the cause, from the kingdom,
recoiling from the intimacy
that I wanted to share with all
as I knelt with bowl and towel.
If you had been there, ask yourself,
what would you have done?

Carol Dixon

The source of happiness

The Gospel according to John gives a different account of Jesus' last Thursday with his followers. In addition to the meal that he shared, Jesus also bent down and washed his disciples' dirty feet. When he was finished, he gave his followers the mandate to do the same – a mandate that we rarely follow. So during this season of Lent, I think it is important to reflect on foot washing and to put it into practice.

At the Open Door we often practise foot washing at our community retreats.

For me, it has become a sacrament every bit as important as baptism and the Lord's Supper. And unlike the Lord's Supper and baptism, I have several specific memories of foot washing.

I remember how awkward I felt the first time I practised foot washing. It was the middle of February, my feet were cold, and I thought it was pretty ridiculous to perform this ritual that no church I had ever attended practised.

But then I was a staid and sedate Lutheran. When it was over I was completely surprised to find that foot washing had become for me a holy ritual with as much, or more, meaning as the Lord's Supper …

Perhaps the strongest impression I have of foot washing is the unsophisticated, uninhibited sense of joy I always experience. Somebody struggles with stifling the giggles as their feet get tickled, but the laughter always wins, and the room fills with happiness.

However, foot washing is not just a laughing matter, and I have often thought about its sacramental qualities. As there is more to the Lord's Supper than a piece of bread and a cup of juice, so there is more to this mandate to wash each other's feet than soap and water. Foot washing is, as are the traditional sacraments, a means of grace instituted by Jesus. Jesus says to his followers, '*I have set an example for you, so that you will do just what I have done for you. I am telling you the truth: no slave is greater than their master, and no messenger is greater than the one who sent them. Now that you know this truth, how happy you will be if you put it into practice!*'

What was it that Jesus did for his followers? It was a fairly amazing, yet simple, act. Jesus, the Lord and Teacher, the master of the slaves, the sender of the messengers, stooped and washed the dirtiest part of his students, his slaves, his messengers. Then he instructed them to do the same for each other, and to learn the truth: that he had sent them to serve the lowly, not those who typically are served. Jesus promises happiness to his followers if they put into practice the truth he has just taught. So there is grace – a fitness, a blessing, a mercy granted – in the simple act of servanthood.

Here we are in Lent with a mandate to serve – not the rich and the powerful (who typically have servants) – but the poor and the oppressed (who typically are servants). How will we know that we are following Jesus' mandate?

Jesus tells us clearly through the gracious gift of joy: *'How happy you will be if you put it into practice!'*

Traditionally, Lent is a time of sadness and mourning. The hymns we sing are somber, telling of Jesus' suffering and death for us. Often we practise a discipline of giving something up for Lent so that, in some small way, through deprivation, we can experience the suffering of Jesus.

Perhaps this Lent we should focus more on Jesus' mandate to practise the truth and to find happiness. Perhaps we should spend this season of Lent reflecting on our daily activities and the happiness in our lives. Is there joy in what we do, or are we merely occupying our time so we can be numb to the dread that fills our days? Do we go to work because it makes us happy, or are we trapped by the need to make money so that we can buy a new car, or a newer, bigger house, or a television, or a computer, or anything else that fills our lives with a false sense of happiness – false because it masks the pain and struggle of our world, false because it is self-serving, false because the desired object might break, or crash with economic failure. Most important, are we serving the poor and the oppressed? That is where we will find happiness, according to Jesus' mandate.

To those of us on top, it seems strange that Jesus would suggest a life of servanthood as the source of happiness. There is much suffering, much pain, and it is felt keenly by the poor, because they cannot buy their way off the street or out of prison; the poor cannot comfort themselves with material goods to forget their struggle. Those who live in service to the poor must know and feel the suffering and pain, too. How can there be happiness where there is suffering and pain? …

Murphy Davis, the Open Door Community

About the Open Door Community (from https://opendoorcommunity.org):

'The Open Door Community, in Baltimore, Maryland, USA, is a residential community in the Catholic Worker tradition (we're sometimes called a Protestant Catholic Worker House). We seek to dismantle racism, sexism and hetero-sexism, abolish the death penalty, and proclaim the Beloved Community through loving relationships with some of the most neglected and outcast of God's children: the homeless and our sisters and brothers who are in prison.

We also advocate on behalf of the oppressed, homeless and prisoners through non-violent protests, grassroots organising and the publication of our monthly newspaper, Hospitality.

We serve breakfast at our Welcome Table every Monday and Wednesday mornings at 9am–10:30am at the Upton Metro Station on the corner of Pennsylvania and Laurens. We are outside in the open area next to the Avenue Market. The breakfast consists of Granola bars, coffee or sweet tea, water, bananas and chicken noodle soup.'

(To read about the Iona Community's connection with the Open Door Community, see 'Open Door Community', by Norman Shanks, and 'The foot clinic', by Ruth Douglas Shanks, in Standing on Our Stories: The Justice, Peace and Wholeness Commitment of the Iona Community, *Susan Dale (Ed.), Wild Goose Publications, 2020.)*

God who washes our feet

God who washes our feet,
God who commands us to love:
before the prayers in the garden,
and the stations of the cross;
before the tomb and the spices
and the stone they put in place,
there was this moment
when you showed us what it meant
to be divine.
May we not forget
that the power to defeat death
was not what you wanted us to imitate.
It was to lay aside all other things
and to love.
Amen.

Corrymeela Community

Love God and one another (even if they have smelly feet)

God says we're all part of each other –
we're all part of this great big worldwide family
and so we're meant to live
together in love and harmony.
But in our family, we fight.
I mean, my brother's OK, right,
but how am I meant to love him –
for a start he has smelly feet.

And as for my sister,
well, she's odd – she dresses
like a goth for a start
and she's always making fun of me.
While dad – he snores (and worse
but we'll not go into that).

And mum nags all the time ...
'Tidy your bedroom, clean your shoes,

put your coat away, don't dirty your best clothes –
I'm not doing any more washing this week …'

Me? I'm perfect (almost),
apart from the fact I'm untidy …
And I always choose the telly programmes
(well, that's not a fault, is it? –
I have impeccable taste).
Of course they love me:
I'm a lovable person.

Well, mum says she does,
and dad, and my sister
sometimes brings me sweets
and my brother lets me share his i-Pod –
as long as I don't mention his smelly feet.

Carol Dixon

Break bread in new fields (A lockdown reflection)

How do we break bread, O Lord,
when we can't kneel together,
pray side by side, clasp hands in peace?

How can we follow your pattern,
remember that evening when
you shared your last meal with friends?

That breaking, crumbling, tearing
of wholesome, lovingly made bread
resonates now, as our hearts break,
crumble and tear alongside friends,
neighbours, strangers, those who

have no bread,
have no jobs,
no company,
whose evenings are long and dark.
We share our hearts with them,

pray for them,
give to them,
send to them
and somehow

a morsel of healing,
a taste of hope,
a sip of comfort
comes to us,

warmed by the love you give us,
the compassion you share with us,
which grows in our communities,
in our spread-out, non-touching church.

Judy Dinnen

Sacrament

On Maundy Thursday, the Christian Church recalls Jesus' final meal with his disciples, when the Sacrament of the Lord's Supper – the Eucharist or Communion – was instituted in the breaking of bread and sharing of wine. A sacrament is something instituted by Jesus as a visible sign and effective channel of the grace of God to all who are open and willing to receive. So, on a day when the fellowship of Holy Communion isn't available to us, because of Covid, what sacrament might we share?

The guidance I received from one of my college tutors, Dr David Lyall, gives us our answer. David talked of the 'pastoral sacrament', a moment of pastoral care which lifts both the giver and the receiver from the human to the divine, and creates a moment of holiness and wonder.

Today, then, why not take time to reflect on the meaning of that sacrament in your life: as nurses care for the sick; as a friend phones you to ask after you and remind you that you're being prayed for; as the pharmacy keeps your prescriptions up to date; as your shopping is delivered to your door; or if you've done anything like that for someone else ... all visible and effective channels of the grace of God.

Sacraments that make us all ministers to one another.

Prayer:

Thank you, God, for all the visible signs of your grace which I will know today. Let me see in them effective channels of your love and blessing. Amen.

Tom Gordon, 2020

One day

One day, we'll step out of doors,
walk down the street, meet our friends,
share a cup of coffee and chocolate cake.

One day we'll play football, build a fire,
roast potatoes, sing a sea shanty, climb a
mountain. We'll open wide church doors.

One day we'll cry for the lost,
remember the stillness and separation
with due respect, carry the candle of calm
into our daily lives, watch with joy,
as petals open, birds build their nests,
bumblebees fly from flower to flower.

We'll remember to stop, be still,
cherish birdsong and new blossom.
We'll cook and converse with new care,
study and travel with eyes open.

We'll pray and praise with new vigour.
We'll break bread with fresh delight.
We'll message, e-mail and Zoom with
new respect, with love and diligence.

Together with friend and stranger,
we'll know our deep humanity,
our links across waves and mountains.
We'll hold hands and share vision.

One day we'll remember and share,
carry the candle of calm into daily life,
respect the stranger, cry for the lost.
One day we'll celebrate our whole world.

Judy Dinnen

GOOD FRIDAY

Praetorium

We batter you with questions,
some of them rhetorical,
as if you are our fall guy, our patsy,
the one against whom we can demonstrate
our superior wit and intelligence.
After all, we already know the answers.

But you remain silent.

Some of us ask,
'What sign will you show us?'
'What miracles will you perform?'
as if you are a dancing bear
there to entertain
or give us all that we crave.

But you remain silent.

Some of us dare to look deeply into
your dark, sad eyes
and know that such questions
are meaningless,
superficial.
Only keeping vigil with you
in your profound silence
will answer the real question
you ask of us:

'Who do you say I am?'
On which all other questions hang.

Rev'd Sr Sandra Sears, CSBC

Mediterranean Hope

'Mediterranean Hope is a project conceived by the Federation of Protestant Churches in Italy. The project began in early 2014 as a response to the challenging situations of Mediterranean migrants. Many refugees are arriving from North Africa, sub-Saharan Africa and the Middle East to the Italian coasts, and in particular, the island of Lampedusa.' (From Mediterranean Hope)

29th September, 2020:

Despite the difficulties and restrictions triggered by Covid-19, people continue to migrate, and the work of Mediterranean Hope goes on. This summer, the clement weather and calm seas have beckoned even more than last summer across the Mediterranean from North Africa.

Those in our Lampedusa-based team are always on hand to provide a welcome to new arrivals, as well as to monitor and report on what is happening there. In a single August weekend when over 400 arrived, migrant numbers swelled to over 1500. Capacity in the 'hotspot' detention centre is for 192. I spent some time on Lampedusa this month and witnessed some of these arrivals for myself, as well as the transfer of migrants from the hotspot to two 'quarantine ships' moored off the island's shores. It was desperate. From afar, the white ferries, nestled in clear turquoise waters just a few hundred metres from bikini-clad holidaymakers, looked just like floating hotels. However, close up, from a vantage point on rocks overlooking the discreet dock where they were moored, the picture was quite different. Minibuses packed with migrants pulled up, their occupants spilling out, each with a plastic bag of personal items. Under the hot sun, they waited (for too long), now socially distanced and masked, before being called, row by row, onto the ships under the watchful eyes of Frontex, the police, UNHCR and the Red Cross. All had already been tested for Covid. However, word has it that, although separated, those who test positive share the boats with those who test negative and that, on at least one boat, the number of positive cases swelled during the quarantine period.

Despite this, the number testing positive amongst the migrant population is said to be tiny, much lower than amongst the population at large. Regrettably, their exposure to overcrowded conditions on arrival increases the risk of contagion. From our team's perspective, it would make more sense for these folk to be transferred directly from Lampedusa to Italy's half-empty reception centres to be quarantined in reasonable conditions and begin the asylum process. Instead, they are stowed temporarily on ferries off Italy's coasts at no small cost to the state. The politics of reception are, however, complex and the messaging associated with the presence of quarantine ships is very clear. For the migrants concerned, the limbo continues: from boat to detention to boat with little clarity as to what the end result will be.

Our advocacy work to reform migration policy and institute the expansion of our humanitarian corridors programme continues. Our bold ambition is to see corridors open across Europe from all fifteen countries along the Central Mediterranean Route, including Libya. That the political obstacles are considerable has not dampened our determination. Meanwhile, our existing corridor from Lebanon to Italy has fallen victim to Covid travel restrictions. We hope that the temporary suspension can be lifted within the next couple of months.

Covid disrupts – but disruption is not always negative. Within the past six months, Italy has been forced to recognise more explicitly the contribution that undocumented seasonal migrant workers make to its economy, and legal reform has extended some limited rights to those in sectors such as agriculture. Within recent days, the government has published its proposals to overturn the notorious 'security decree' spearheaded by Matteo Salvini during his tenure as Minister of the Interior. I suspect that neither of these changes would have been possible within this time-frame had we not all been forced to see things from a very different perspective. There is still much to do but, as I said at the outset, the work goes on ...

Fiona Kendall, European and Legal Affairs Advisor of Mediterranean Hope (www.mediterraneanhope.com)

Remembering

Lord,
you who knew suffering;
may I be still for a moment
and remember
all who today are
silenced
violated
imprisoned
cheated
abused
driven from home
exploited
held hostage
robbed

tortured
rejected
betrayed
marginalised
tyrannised
detained without trial
despised
persecuted
abandoned
killed ...

Peter Millar

The cloak

Years ago
someone laid a cloak on my shoulders –
an unloving parent,
abusive teacher,
the school bully ...
Most of the time I don't even think about it,
but lately I have become aware
of its suffocating heaviness.

You'd think that after all this time
it would have worn thin,
this second skin.
But still it weighs on me,
bowing me down.

Who will strip it from me?

Lord, many years ago
they tried to vest you with such a cloak,
all the while jeering and taunting,
demanding that you live down to their expectations.
But you refused to let it settle;
choosing dignity over bullying,
you took it all to the cross.

Forgiving all, you shrugged it off,
and stood tall enough
to reach heaven.

Please teach me how to do that,
how to forgive.
How to shrug this cloak off.
How to stand up straight and tall
and look you in the eye.

Rev'd Sr Sandra Sears, CSBC

Denial

I told him I'd die for him, you know,
that night in the upper room,
and I meant it. He just looked at me
with that knowing smile of his,
and slightly shook his head, while his eyes
bored into my soul with such love
as he said he knew I wouldn't.
I didn't believe him, of course –
none of us did – we were all so sure
of ourselves, our faith in him,
in the future.

Even later on, standing in the courtyard
by the flickering firelight, when I denied
I knew him, it was like someone else
speaking, it couldn't be me.
Or so I thought, until he looked at me

as they brought him out, battered, bruised,
draped in the purple robe, with that cruel crown
on his bleeding head, like a parody
of a puppet king.

They say Pilate asked him if he was a king.
I wouldn't know. I don't speak Latin or Greek,
but John knew the interpreter –
John has quite a few friends in high places,
which was how we came to be in the courtyard
in the first place, standing by the charcoal fire.
Every time I smell one now, I remember.

I told him I'd die for him;
yet, when it came to it,
I suppose he died for me,
for all of us.
What kind of king does that?

Carol Dixon

Veronica's gift

My life is woven cloth:
imperfect,
disfigured at times
by unloveliness;
but it is all I have to offer.
And this I do,
tearfully,
only to find it hallowed
by the imprint of your face.

Rev'd Sr Sandra Sears, CSBC

Under the cross

Lord,
I have fallen yet again
under the weight of this cross.
I lie here,
mouth full of dirt,
so it is impossible to even pray.
But then I see
that you are lying beside me,
head next to mine,
bleeding from your crown of thorns.

'Rest here with me for a while,
then we can both move on,
caring for each other's pain.'

And then the cross becomes bearable
once again,
and I can hope once more
for resurrection
after the struggle.

Rev'd Sr Sandra Sears, CSBC

He was held down (A prayer of confession)

He was held down,
one kneeling on him,
pinioning each arm ...
Nails were driven
into his flesh,
while he lay helpless
on the hard ground.
People standing by
looked on, helpless
in the face of authority,
as he gasped,
'Father, forgive them,

for they know not
what they do.'

Father, forgive us
for each time
we condone
injustice and hate,
allow mob rule
and violence to prevail,
or stand idly by
while those in authority
go unchallenged;
when we refuse to forgive,
forget to bring your peace
and love for all to the world,
for each time we do,
Christ is crucified again.

Carol Dixon

Crucifix

Lord,
let me be the wood
against which you are crucified.
Let the nails which pierce your hands and feet
be driven into me.
Let me learn your obedience
in the face of death;
your forgiveness
in the midst of horror,
and let my arms stretch out with yours
to gather the whole world
into your loving embrace.
Amen.

Rev'd Sr Sandra Sears, CSBC

Breathe 2

In 2020 the act of breathing took on new significance for two reasons. Firstly, a respiratory disease identified in Wuhan, China became a global pandemic. Secondly, 'I can't breathe' (the final words of a black man named George Floyd who was murdered by a police officer) became a protest cry for those looking to end systemic racism in the U.S., the UK and elsewhere. These two events prompted me to look closer at the symbolism of breathing/suffocation in a range of political issues, using brief snapshots into the lives of five characters to do so.

Try to keep breathing Father, even if it's the last thing you do. In

and out. The seeping smog never really cleared, but the children of the inner-city are taught not to see it. Those with asthma are usually twice as likely to have an attack as their middle-class cousins, but with the factories abandoned they breathe a freshness never felt in their throats before, like iced water after football practice. In

and out. A princess climbs to the height of her tower block, a Bag for Life balancing on each of her fishhook fingers. Nipping out for a few things has become an act of violence so she carries seven days of rations to her children, carriageless. Panting upon the pale air, she manages the final flight – a word wholly unreflective of this scramble – and collapses. In

and out. Breathe knowing that somewhere a green thing is holding your breath safe for you, protecting your children from the gases you exhale – that growing goddess, that green lung turning black as a smoker's. In

and out. An NHS nurse and her skeleton crew catch at breaths escaping like balloons while back home in the Eastern Cape South Africa sick people are fighting over dwindling medical supplies. They are afraid the same will happen here. In

and out. Breathe like George Floyd couldn't, corruption kneeling on his throat. There is no metaphor I can imagine for what that must have been like, but I know it was nothing like how I am kneeling before you now.

Father, why did it take a respiratory disease for us to realise that none of us could really breathe all along?

Matt Sowerby, Church Action on Poverty

God of the crowds crying, 'Crucify!'

God of the crowds crying, 'Crucify!'
God on the cross crying, 'Forgive them':
by doing and not doing,
we have repeated that Friday scene
in countless ways,
in countless places,
to countless sons and daughters.
We know not what we do
even when we know too well.
We are now facing death in a new way.
And human frailty. And human need.
And human solidarity.
Perhaps as we begin to see as you see
the reality of who we are,
we can finally begin to love as you love,
answer compassionately the cries we hear,
and be able to forgive, ourselves.
Amen.

Corrymeela Community

The mother

John 19:26

She looked at him
and saw that he was dying,
and rebelled against the futility of it all.
Already he seemed
so far away from her,
like a stranger, almost.
She had known him
little more than
thirty years, such
a short time really
in the aeons of eternity.

The emptiness which filled
her heart was replaced
by a kind of repugnance
as she looked at him –
a shadow of his former self –
his bleeding, sweating body
racked with pain; it was
revolting, repellent,
disgusting. Where was the glory
and majesty of death
which people talked about?

She shut her eyes
to try to efface the horror
of it all …… and saw
the stable and the blood
upon the straw, recalled
the stench of sweat
and warm animals –
felt their hot breath and the pain
of the child fighting
its way out of her womb –
from the darkness
into Light!

Looking up, she caught his eye
and, meeting his tranquil gaze,
understood he knew that they
had travailed this journey before.
The ghastly gore of death
was no different to that of birth.
The glory came afterwards …

'It is accomplished!'
he cried to the world;
and she smiled, through
the mists of her tears.

Carol Dixon

Deposition

It is finished.
Three long, agonising hours
have passed. It is finished.
Jesus himself said so,
and hung his head.

It is finished.
The hopes, the dreams,
the longings. All finished.
Only the shell of a once
vibrant body remains;
limp and useless as his
disciples' dreams.

The body cut down.
Limp as a scarecrow.
Passed to his disciples;
helpless now all hope has died.

It is finished.
His mother, elderly now, worn out,
stooped, limp and finished,
takes her son's tired body
and wraps it once more
in swaddling cloths,
and lays him in the tomb as once
she laid him in the manger.

S Anne Lawson

Here and now

O Jesus, you weren't only crucified 2000 years ago.
You are being crucified today –
here and now ...

We pray for those who are being crucified here and now:

We pray for those being crucified by poverty:
in Somalia, in Easterhouse in Glasgow, in Birmingham ...
For victims of capitalism and other Powers;
for those struggling under the burden of unfair debt and trade,
unfair debt and trade we profit by.

We pray for children being crucified.
Children working in sweatshops around the world.
Children who make the clothes we wear,
who help to harvest the food we eat.

We pray for women being crucified.
Women working in the sex trade in London, in Bangkok ...
Women who suffer abuse in our neighbourhoods
and in the neighbourhood of the world.
Women who suffer while we look away, deny, remain silent.

We pray for those being crucified by disease,
by AIDS, TB, malaria ...
Diseases which might be cured or better-treated
if only we'd choose life;
if only, as a nation,
we didn't spend 30 billion pounds every year
on the military;
if only, as a world,
we didn't spend over one trillion dollars U.S. a year
on war and death.
And we pray that vaccines for Covid are quickly and freely
made available to all people in poor countries around the world
and that we in the West don't hoard them.[1]

We pray for political prisoners and prisoners of conscience
being crucified in jails around the world:

in Saudi Arabia, the Philippines, China, Hong Kong ...
in countries and by countries whose governments
our government is often happy to do business with
and to call friends.

And we pray for the good earth,
this precious, fragile home
we pay mock homage,
give poisoned streams to drink,
bind with fences,
strip and beat and flog and
pierce with spears
until the blood and water pours out.

Jesus Christ,
we confess our complicity in all these crucifixions,
and in others.
Forgive us, Lord, we don't know what we're doing.
Or do we?

We give thanks for individuals and organisations
working to bring healing and
hope in your world:

Church Action on Poverty
Oxfam
Save the Children
Christian Aid
Médecins Sans Frontières
Amnesty International
Greenpeace ...

(Name or think of other organisations, groups ...)

We give thanks for their passion and commitment.

Spirit of love,
help us to do all we can to support them in their work;
help us to do more to ease suffering and to bring healing and hope
in our neighbourhoods and in the neighbourhood of the world.

Christ has no other hands but our hands:
No other hands but our hands
to do God's work in the world.
Christ has no love but our love:
No love but our love to share with
the imprisoned, the silenced,
the persecuted, the marginalised …
Amen.

Neil Paynter

1. *There are a number of petitions, actions on the Internet concerning this.*

Cross in the bus station

In Jerusalem on the
east side there is a
bus station
below a rocky
outcrop which
in ancient times
they called
the place of the skull.
Here, some say,
they crucified him,
not on top
of the hill perhaps
but at ground level,
among the city's
teeming commerce
near a public
rubbish dump.
Here where people
come and go
they pinned him
down.
From here, he is set free
to travel the world.

Warren R Bardsley

This is not the end: A reflection and meditation for Good Friday

Bible readings:

> *'My God, my God, why have you forsaken me?
>   Why are you so far from helping me, from the words of my groaning?'*
>
> *(Psalm 22:1, NRSV)*
>
> *From noon on, darkness came over the whole land until three in the afternoon. And about three o'clock Jesus cried with a loud voice, 'Eli, Eli, lema sabachthani?' that is, 'My God, my God, why have you forsaken me?' …*
>
> *Then Jesus cried again with a loud voice and breathed his last.*
>
> *(Matthew 27:45–46, 50, NRSV)*

Today is the darkest day.

Today we remember Judas' betrayal.

Today we hear the crowds crying for Jesus' death,
and we feel Pilate's weakness and fear.

Today we feel the weight of the cross,
the sharpness of the crown of thorns and the pain of the nails.

Today we hear again of the last hours of Jesus' life.

Today we remember with sorrow the crucifixion and death of Jesus.

Today we hear and feel Jesus giving his life for us.

Today is heartbreaking.

Today, despite knowing the glorious happy ending,
we shed tears of grief.

Today is the darkest day.

My God, my God, why have you forsaken me? …

I wrote this poem a few years ago, at a time when I was unwell and suffering with pain. For the first time, I felt physically connected to the suffering of Jesus on the cross.

This year I'm inviting you to put yourself into Jesus' place, to sit at the foot of the cross and feel as he felt; to feel as his disciples and mother felt.

Before you start reading the following meditation, take a few deep breaths, remembering that God is with you.

Now read these words slowly, allowing them to settle with you:

Jesus is nailed to the cross.
Through his hands.
Through his feet.
The pain is unbelievable.
Jesus knows this pain is the last pain for him.

Jesus does not get angry.
He looks at the soldiers who have hurt him
and he asks for God to forgive them.
He looks at his mother, at Mary.
He asks her to look after his disciples,
and asks them to look after her.
Jesus is still thinking about everyone else.

How do you feel?
Do you feel the pain?
The sadness?
Would you be so selfless?
Could you think of others?
We are often wounded by painful words.
Do we think of those people, and ask for them to be forgiven?
Do you find it easy to forgive?

Today you are invited to stay at the foot of the cross
and to ask Jesus to help you:

Help you to love your neighbour.
Help you to forgive people who have hurt you.
Help you to care for those in need.
Help you to stand up to injustice.
Help you to be the best you can be.
Ask Jesus to show you how:
he will guide you every day of your life.

This is not the end.
This is just the beginning.

Amen.

Emma Major

Holy Saturday

Unravelling

Jesus,
when you went down to Hades
to preach to the dead,
did you find Judas?
Did you unravel his guilt like a woman's hair*
with your silent, deep eyes?

And will we find him in heaven?
And if we do, will we, Simon-like,
be scandalised?

Or will our unravellings greet his
with a holy kiss?

Rev'd Sr Sandra Sears, CSBC

*Luke 7:36-50

Not just another Saturday

I rarely went to the hospice on a Saturday. Weekends which, for a parish minister, had been the focus of the working week for twenty years, had become family time, me time, R&R time. For a hospice chaplain, work was for weekdays, not weekends. But this Saturday, I had to go in. I can't remember why. Collecting something, probably, on my way into town. Five minutes …

But I didn't expect to be dealing with Brendan.

The Ward Sister saw me. 'Tom?' she said. 'It's a Saturday, so why …?'

'Flying visit,' I offered.

'Listen,' she said conspiratorially, 'now you're here, you couldn't pop in to see Brendan, could you? His niece is with him. She's been asking if you were around. I said it was Saturday, but …'

Two minutes later I was at Brendan's bedside, introducing myself to a forlorn woman sitting by the bed. 'Carla, Brendan's niece, from Leicester,' she said. 'You've been good to my uncle Brendan, Father Tom,' she whispered.

I'd been as good with a lovely man as anyone had been. But the 'Father Tom' part? I didn't correct her. 'Nice to meet you, Father Tom,' Brendan had said the first time we'd met. There was no point in correcting him. It made a douce Presbyterian feel kind of warm inside. Father Tom ... I never corrected Brendan when he asked to join a small Communion service I'd arranged for a few patients, even though I reminded him it wasn't a Catholic Mass. 'Nae bother, Father Tom,' he'd replied. I never corrected him when he asked me to pray the Lord's Prayer him and he said 'trespasses' when I said 'debts', and he said, 'Sorry, Father Tom.' I never corrected him when he introduced me to all and sundry by my new title. And now his niece too ...

Suddenly, Carla took my hand. 'Father Tom,' she said, 'would you give Communion to my uncle? I know you've done it before. He told me that.'

I thought of the different ways I could respond ... not a priest ... no time ... nothing ready ... busy ward ... not properly dressed ... it's a Saturday ... But I heard myself saying, 'OK. And do you want Communion too?'

'Not me, Father Tom,' she replied. 'I'm off outside for a fag!'

I was in the kitchen when the Ward Sister came in. 'I thought it was a flying visit,' she said, 'it being a Saturday ...'

'Oh, just getting Communion organised for Brendan,' I replied.

'Communion?' she responded ... 'But he's unconscious. He'll not know you're there. There's no point.'

'But ... well ...' I muttered.

'OK. But don't take long. We've got the lunches to do in ten minutes.'

I pulled the screens round Brendan's bed for the ten-minute Communion and looked at the unconscious old man. Sister was right, I thought. What is the point of this ... and on a Saturday? I put the Communion elements on Brendan's bedside table, opened my prayer book to the right page, and said, 'The Grace of the Lord Jesus Christ be with us all.' And Brendan opened his eyes. He blinked a few times is if he was trying to focus. And then, catching my eye, he said in a faint but discernible whisper, 'Father Tom?' I didn't correct him, but smiled in recognition. 'Communion?' he said.

'Yes, Brendan,' I replied, barely able to speak.

The Communion took a good deal less than ten minutes. A crumb of bread in the corner of his mouth. A drop of wine on a little sponge across his lips. The Lord's Prayer said together, with me getting it right with the 'trespasses' bit. And the blessing.

'The Lord be with you,' I concluded. 'And also with you, Father Tom,' Brendan said quietly, and closed his eyes again.

I was pulling the screens back when the Ward Sister appeared with the lunch trolley. 'How'd you get on?' she asked. I had nothing to say. She looked down at the sleeping Brendan. 'I told you you'd get nothing out of him today.' I didn't correct her. But, when I left the hospice, it wasn't on 'just another Saturday'. A moment of holiness had changed everything.

When I got back to work on the Monday, I learned that Brendan had died on the Saturday night. 'He wasn't supposed to,' one of the nurses said. 'And he was so much more peaceful than he'd been for days,' said another. 'Must have been the medication,' said a third.

I didn't correct her. For I knew that Brendan and Father Tom had been touched by mystery and wonder that had changed our lives, by a blessing on what had been nothing less than our Holy Saturday.

Tom Gordon

Suggestions for reflection and action on Holy Saturday

Spend time today in a cemetery or graveyard.

Tend the grave of a family member, a friend, or a stranger.

Give yourself time and permission to grieve:
for someone you love,
for lost opportunities,
for unfulfilled dreams.

Ask yourself:
What has or needs to die in me this year?
Who or what holds me captive?

What is God raising to life in me?
In my home? In my community?

Explore how the harrowing of Hell has been portrayed
in art, drama and story.

Somewhere in your home, clean, oil or possibly paint a door.
Focus on the divine activity of opening and closing doors.
Pray as you work.

Ruth Burgess

A Saturday of waiting

'It's about waiting,' they said.
'It takes time,' they said.
'It doesn't happen overnight,' they said.
'You'll have to be patient,' they said.
They all said it, in different ways.
It was their way, right enough.
I knew it was true; I'd said so myself.
But I didn't like the waiting time.

The death had been so hard.
The run-up to it, even though I knew.
The awfulness of it, even though I was ready.
The finality of it, even though I believed.
So, we laid him to rest, yesterday.
Cold, it was, and empty by his grave.
But we did it, on a Friday morning.
And it wasn't good; no Good Friday for me.

And now, it's about waiting, just as they said.
A nothing time; a passing time;
an empty time; a wasted time;
a time between what was and what could be …
This time, my time, to be patient,
between my hellish Friday and … what?
A new life? An Easter morn?
No, I don't see that, or, at least, not yet.

So, it's my Saturday of waiting.
My holy Saturday? Oh, that it would be so …
But instead, it's my in-between Saturday,
my waiting-for-something-to-come-along Saturday.
My Saturday of endless, empty hours;
this day of functioning, and not living;
frozen in time, between the before and after;
the grind of not knowing why or how or when.

So I wait, just as they said.
It'll take time, just as I always knew.
It won't happen overnight, just as I'd been told.
I'll have to be patient, for I have no choice.
It's my Saturday of waiting, my day of existing.
Holy or hellish, it makes little odds.
It just has to be lived through, expectantly,
till living comes along again tomorrow.

Tom Gordon

Death cafés 2020

Many cafés this year
were regrettably
not places where
you could sit at tables
or sprawl on sofas
and share stories and questions
about life and death.

Park benches could be dodgy too,
and it was better
never to speak face to face.

Masks hid our features,
emotions were hard to read.
Hugs were very definitely out.

Death and life was all around us:
on the daily news

in our communities
among our families and friends.

Loss was huge.

Maybe
sometime
in 2021
we can again share stories
and ask questions
and learn from each other
in real cafés
with coffee
and lots of cake.

Ruth Burgess

For information on death cafés, see: https://deathcafe.com

God of grieving

God of grieving,
God of silence,
there is a strange gift in having time,
one whole day this holy week,
to sit with questions of why and how long
and to hear no response at all.
To rush from Friday to Sunday,
from death to resurrection,
wouldn't do either justice.
Nor would it dignify the life of those
whose daily pain and grief
and constant pleas for justice
go unanswered in the world's daily rhythm.
Let your silence fill this silence,
until our empty noise dies out.
Amen.

Corrymeela Community

Easter Sunday

A garden-grave

Swathed now, as swaddled once,
Love-wound in grief,
Wounded in grief,
Constrained in brief mortality
For hours only.
The tomb gapes for him, then
Stone runs its grating groove
Of finality.
    The guard is set.

A day, long as a thousand years.

The women watch and wait,
Marking the sun's setting and rising, setting
And rising,
Then, they may rise
And go to the place, seeking to mend
With tenderness gashes of lash, thorn, nail.

But in the secret darkness,
Light. Light dissolving grave clothes,
Flinging aside windings of head and neck
With earth-shaking laughter. Striding irresistible
Through stone, through ancient groves
Of Gethsemane garden
To that other garden,
Turning time backwards, to dawn, to beginning,
Releasing time's captives, plundering death.

And now, in the still and opal light of morning,
Waiting for his friends, waiting to mend
Their fear of death,
The rift of shame and grief,
Their desperate weariness.
To say, 'It is the end
Of all that was past.
My breath is life;
This rising, light and lightness, is my gift.'

Janet Killeen

Fake news – a soldier speaks (Matthew 28:11–15)

We wasn't asleep, sir. I swear by all the gods we wasn't.
It would be more than our life's worth, sir,
to fall asleep while we're on duty.
I know we should've been standin' guard but it was cold
and we huddled together wrapped in our cloaks.
But we had all our weapons to hand, sir,
if anyone had come upon us sudden-like.
You want to know what happened?
Well, sir, I don't rightly know.
One minute we was sittin' there like I said,
and the next there was this bright light
and we was flat on our backs on the ground –
as though somethin' from the gods had struck the earth.

I suppose it could have been an earthquake, sir.
Just like the other day – my friend on duty
at that crucifixion said he'd never seen or felt the like
when all went dark as that man died.
And I did hear that your Temple was damaged as well.
Maybe last night was a bit of an aftershock.
You hear about them from time to time.

What did we see?
Well, as I said, sir, there was this bright light,
then there were like two shining figures
and it looked as though another joined them
from out the tomb. I didn't rightly see, sir,
we was blinded and shocked as you can imagine.

What's that, sir?
We could never say it was his mates
came and snatched the body.
We'd be done for dereliction of duty.
Oh, you've squared it with the governor.
That's all right then. And very kind of you
to give us a little something, sir.
Our pay these days doesn't go far.

Right you are, sir.
It's as good as a wink and a nod
to a blind horse, as they say.
Yes, sir. It must have been his followers
that hoodwinked us with all their devilry.
You never know what these people
will get up to next!

Carol Dixon

Daybreak

Gently, she let her footsteps take her back
To yesterday, leaving the household sleeping,
Scoured by grief, but burnished now with joy.
The dark sky, splintered with stars, waited
For the sun to run a burning finger
Along the rim of the earth.
Trees whispered of their guardianship of time.
Then, a sudden rush of shimmering brightness,
Birdsong, and a shivering breeze.

Here, at the maw of rock,
She had flung her desperate question,
And heard it answered.
Here she had been named, known,
As in a pristine moment, God had so named Adam.
Then Adam, Woman,
While creatures gathered to them, to receive
Each marvellous identity.
She, too, had found her true self, named and called
To endless possibility.
The earth, silver and green and gold,
Had sprung afresh to life. New made. Unfurled.

That daybreak, beneath ancient trees
Rooted in springs deeper than memory,
She saw how Resurrection bathed the world in light,
To heal its age-embittered wounds and shames.

She understood: this radiance
Could transform its weariness with life;
Its peoples quicken to eternal playfulness,
Their garden-given innocence restored.

Janet Killeen

'Noli me tangere' (John 20:17)

I don't want you to go, Lord!
Don't leave me by myself again.
I need to feel you near me all the time,
your reassuring presence with me.
I thought I'd lost you forever
and now I've found you again,
I can't bear to let you go.

Jesus says:
'Do not cling to me,
I have to go to others
who need me just as much
as you, or more;
and if you dare to let me go
you'll find I'm with you
always, everywhere,
to the edge of eternity …
and beyond.

Carol Dixon

God of unbounded joy

God of unbounded joy,
God of undying love:
the women went to the tomb
to tend to the crucified dead
and came back the first preachers
of resurrection.
As we come back from our tomb today,

and begin to live again,
may we deliver with unbridled joy
what the world is dying to hear:
that death is never the end;
that love remains what is most divine;
and that you continue to live
in the beating heart of our humanity.
Amen.

Corrymeela Community

A matter of where you're standing

Spring, where I come from,
is the wrong way up.
Just like the country.
Northerners can't understand
how Easter can be seen
through our autumn eyes.
It's easy for them.
The long winter has been cruelly cold,
the ice and snow have finally melted,
and the struggling spring sun
brings relief for aching arthritic bodies.
Where trees were bare
and fields bleak with frost,
leaves and flowers erupt
in a brilliant show
of blossom
and greenery.

What better way to herald
the story of
the spectacular rising
of our Lord
after such long, cruel torment.

But,
believe it or not,
it's the same for us.

There's been no rain
since November,
and the searing heat
has brought bushfires,
fanned by blustery winds from the north,
straight from the parched desert.
Nothing can grow under those conditions,
and we long for relief.
And then …
and then …
mid-February/early March,
the wind shifts south and west,
bringing coolness,
and with it,
rain.
And the smell of it!
Ah, the smell of it –
and the sound of it on the tin roof!
There is no sweeter sound!

And within hours
green whiskers are showing in the paddocks.
Within days gardens are erupting
into a cacophony of colour.
As Christ endured
the searing heat
of lies and betrayal and abuse,
and white-hot pain
of tearing thorns and nails,
the coolness of the tomb
was just the thing
to nurture this broken, dead seed
into spectacular new life.
So you see,
there's not much difference between us.

It's just a matter of
where you happen to be standing.

Rev'd Sr Sandra Sears, CSBC

The rising tide (Reflection on Easter Day 2020)

'A rising tide lifts all boats.'

Aphorism used by U.S. President John F Kennedy

The working harbour in Port Seton, the village on the Forth where I live, gives you all the evidence you need of the truth of the proverb above. Whether the incoming tide, brought by a wild gale, is a fierce one which crashes over the walls, or a gentle one, which slowly floods the inner harbour, the result is the same. The rising tide lifts all boats, large and small, up to the quayside, so that stores can be loaded, nets readied and creels prepared for the fishermen to set out to sea when the tide is right.

On this Easter Day, a day so dramatically different from any other Easter we've experienced in our lifetime, what's to be said? 'The Lord is risen; He is risen indeed' will still ring out from the Christian Church – over the airwaves; in podcasts; in private homes; in the hearts of Easter people. And we give thanks to God that the Easter message is not diminished by our world in crisis – today of all days.

We may struggle to believe that, or, indeed, we may believe it in our hearts but doubt it in our minds. So, I offer you this thought ... Just as the rising tide lifts all boats, so our message of 'rising' this Easter will be a tide that lifts us all. We may not know it, or believe it, or understand it. But the message of hope, the message that the grave will not have its victory, will raise us all up to the quayside once again.

The boats don't have to understand the rising tide to get the benefit of it. They just give themselves to the seas and they'll be lifted anyway. The rising tide will lift all boats – yours and mine among them.

Prayer:

God of Easter Day, let the promise of your rising not just be for the Church to celebrate, but let it also be for me. Raise me up. Set me straight. Make me ready. Give me hope. Lift me high. Prepare me to set sail again when the tide is right. Amen.

Tom Gordon

On the road

The road to Emmaus

It was unrealistic, I suppose, hoping everything would change,
for something huge, remarkable, to come about,
expecting that our land, our people, would be freed.
We thought he had the answer; we followed him in anticipation
of a world transformed, of everything made new;
and trusted he could do it.

We left Jerusalem; now nothing there for us –
no triumph, no glory or rejoicing,
just a ravaged body on a cross
(in spite of talk of angels in the tomb).
We trudged the road, stumbling, reliving
the disappointment, grief – and wondering 'what now?'
Hopes dashed, old hurts resurfacing.
Back to the way it was.

There are always other travellers on the road.
We weren't good company, but this man
joined us anyway, curious to hear what we were saying
as we went over it again; he seemed nice enough.
We thought he would have heard; how could he not?
So, wearily, we told him of the trial, the execution,
the empty tomb.

And he began to say how foolish we both were
in not believing what the prophets said.
(Cleophas, at first, was mortified – he hates to be found lacking
in his knowledge of the scriptures; that's men for you.)
But I'd heard the talk of women in the city –
a few had hope that Jesus was somewhere –
though now it seemed
an empty dream.

We wanted to hear more from our companion,
and since we were returning home,
and he was a stranger in the town,
invited him to stay and eat with us,
and not continue on his journey
as night fell.

Then at the meal he said a prayer,
and broke the bread, in such a way –
and passed it round, as if he were the host.
And suddenly we knew, without a doubt,
just who he was.

Then he was gone.

And leaving home once more, retracing steps,
we hurried to Jerusalem – despite our blistered feet –
and found all changed,
that Simon, too, had seen,
had found again our Lord,
as we had in the breaking of the bread.

Jill Rhodes

Dear diary

This poem is based upon a well-known bus route in Sheffield. I thought it would be interesting to set a 'story' on that bus journey as a way of talking about inequality. I wanted to explore how life could be different after Covid-19 and what that may look like on an ordinary day, through an everyday conversation in Sheffield.

I travelled on the 83 bus today, no facemask needed.
It feels like so long ago since we had to wear them.
Covid-19 is a distant memory now.

A woman sat next to me.
We got talking, as you do.
We do that well round here.

She grew up near here.
Turns out that our parents were in the same class at school.
She struggled during Covid.
She ran her own hairdressing business.
Universal Credit took a while to kick in.
Family and friends helped her through, as best they could.
'Never thought I would need to claim though.
I had my own business.'

We sit and look out of the window.
'A few years ago, this bus was in the paper,' she tells me.
'If you follow the route of this bus, people born in some areas have a life expectancy 10 years more than others.
Imagine that.
It's not right.'

But since Covid, things got better.
People didn't just hand out food.
They campaigned.
They shared stories.
For once, people in power finally listened.

She pressed the bell,
said goodbye,

gave me a card.
'If you need a haircut, here's my number.
My business started up again.
But, I don't work on a Friday. I volunteer on that day.'

Charlotte Killeya, Church Action on Poverty

Travelling

Our road cut between ash-grey hills,
Blurring as the sun collapsed to the west.
Our feet were urgent, desperate for home,
Yet stumbling with the dread of a cold hearth,
The morning's bread dry,
The wine sour in a shrunken wineskin.
We talked, words half-expressed,
Thoughts unformed, as though
There were no true words left, no coherent Word,
Fragments only. Companions, shoulder to shoulder,
Yet alone, bewildered, in the separateness of grief.
Sometimes, a pang of hope, from the absurdity
Of the morning's news, but
Always the undertow of disbelief.
We did not hear the following footsteps
Scuffing the dust, hurrying to overtake us,
Until the voice spoke,
Questions, as though we had been overheard
In all our doubts and sadness.
A stranger to us, whose patient answers
Turned slowly to brimming laughter
At our bafflement,
Our incredulity.
He came with us, our fellow-traveller,
To share our paucity of hospitality;
We recognised him then, as the stale bread broke,
Transformed to blessing in the vibrant hands.

Janet Killeen

Two roads

Yesterday I headed to the Second Crematorium south of Taipei to participate in the funeral of a wonderful friend and mentor. I met Dr Samuel Jang, an elder at the East Gate Presbyterian Church in Taipei, twenty-three years ago when we worked together leading an English Bible study for that congregation. I was studying Mandarin at the time, so it was a gift to me to be able to lead a Bible study in English.

Dr Jang was a man who had a contagious joy. He became a Christian in China when he was very young. He went through a lot when China and Japan were at war, and then managed to come to Taiwan, where he continued his medical studies. He became a dentist. He married a Taiwanese and they had four children who all continue to walk in Christ's way. Dr Jang always shared his faith with his patients. He enjoyed teaching children in Sunday school and always told the other teachers that if they had a problem student to let that student join his class. He would then make that student the head of the class. The student was so busy helping Dr Jang, he or she had no time to make trouble. Many of these students, now adults, are the elders and deacons of East Gate Church. Dr Jang's wife had a stroke and was bedridden for fourteen years. He cared for her with love and never complained.

The Second Crematorium in Taipei is huge. It is where the majority of cremations are done in the city. There are at least 15 chapels which cater to Buddhists, Taoists and Christians. The staff at the crematorium are adept at quickly changing these chapels with the symbols of each religion.

I arrived a little early for the service for Dr Jang and noticed about 60 young men all dressed in black T-shirts. Dr Jang's service was to be in the Number 1 Chapel on the third floor and these youth were all congregating at the Number 4 Chapel on the same floor. I asked someone who they were, and was told that they were part of a gang. Gangs in Taiwan are called the Dark Way.

I decided to walk down the hall and meet some of these young gang members. I rarely wear a clerical collar, but had one on yesterday for Dr Jang's service. When I walked up to this group of youth, they seemed surprised (understandably!). I asked a few of them how old they were, and most of them were in their late teens. I surmised that most of them had dropped out of school. When I asked whose funeral they were attending, they didn't answer, as if they were not supposed to answer. But a few of them opened up and told me a little about themselves.

I thought back to two weeks before, when I was speaking at a joint aboriginal youth service. The youth there were about the same age as these young men. And yet the road they are walking is so dramatically different. Gang life here involves drugs and violence. These young men are being used by others. Their future will not be bright.

I then walked back down the hall to participate in the service giving thanks for Dr Jang and the life he lived, and witnessing to our hope in the Resurrection. I thought about Dr Jang's willingness to come alongside troubled students, and so wished that these young men had positive role models in their lives.

As I stood to talk at the service, I couldn't help but compare what was happening in those two chapels. A dark road and a road of light. And I shared that Dr Jang's life is a challenge to all of us, to come alongside those who lead difficult lives. We can accept them and not judge. We can share the love of Christ, who knows their situations so much better than we do.

Two roads. I ask you to pray for these young men and so many around the world who are lured into a life which does not bring life. May we find ways to help them find life.

John McCall, associate member of the Iona Community in Taiwan, from a letter

The other one

You know the story.
The newly risen Christ walked alongside two disciples
on the road to Emmaus.
When he asked them what they were discussing,
one of them, named Cleopas, spoke to him.

Well,
I'm the other one.
If I told you my name
it would mean nothing to you.
When, years later,
they told Luke the story,
they remembered Cleopas,
but forgot me.
Not surprising really.
I never went on a missionary journey,
or founded a church,
or served as an elder or deacon.
I tried to live a good Christian life,
kept my head down during persecution.
In the world's eyes, I'm a nobody.

So, I remember with humble amazement
that the eternal Word of God,
for whom and by whom all things were made,
the Messiah,
the Lamb of God,
the Saviour of all humankind,
chose to spend several hours
trudging along a dusty road,
patiently explaining it all
to Cleopas …
and me.

Brian Ford

Drift anchor (Reflection after Easter Day 2020)

'We have an anchor that keeps the soul
Steadfast and sure while the billows roll,
Fastened to the Rock which cannot move,
Grounded firm and deep in the Saviour's Love.'

Priscilla Jane Owens, from the hymn 'Will your anchor hold?' (1882)

Knowing how hard Easter was going to be this year, I'd prepared this 'Thought for the Day' a couple of weeks ago, to offer encouragement to people by reflecting on the positive aspects of Easter. But, the reality of our situation, and the feelings it has created in me, have caused me to revise this piece in the light of the thoughts I'm left with after Easter Day.

I wanted to say that Easter has confirmed I have an anchor *'fastened to the Rock which cannot move'*; that my anchor was *'grounded firm and deep'* in my faith; that I feel more *'steadfast and sure'*. But I'm not sure I can. One day – perhaps soon – I know I will be able to. But not yet. So, what am I left with after Easter?

Sailors locally tell me that there's such a thing as a drift anchor – a sea anchor or a boat brake. It's a device that's dropped overboard in heavy weather so that the boat can be stabilised and slowed down. Rather than binding the boat to the seabed with a conventional anchor, a drift anchor creates drag and acts as a brake. It's normally attached to a boat's bow and it stops the boat turning side-on to the waves and being overwhelmed by them.

Today, I don't feel I have the big anchor I hoped Easter would provide. I know it's there, for I've used it before, and I'm certain it will work again. But, for now, I'll have to rely on the drift anchor that's been chucked into the sea – my family, friends, church, community, personal resilience – to slow me down, and to make sure I'm not totally overwhelmed. Thank God that, today, I have a drift anchor; that will have to be enough for now.

Prayer:

Ever-present God: Will my anchor hold? Yes, I do believe it will. But it looks like I may have to drift for a bit before I feel completely safe. Amen.

Tom Gordon

These are the feet

Read this piece slowly.

These are the feet that were immersed in the Jordan,
and baptised by John and blessed by God.

These are the feet of the One who wandered the wilderness,
tortured and beaten by the devil for 40 days.

These are the feet that stood in the synagogue:
'Today this scripture is fulfilled in your hearing.'

These are the feet that walked up the Galilean hillside,
followed by crowds to hear the words:
'Blessed are the peacemakers, for they will be called children of God.'

These are the feet of the One who stood as loaves and fish were blessed,
then fed the world.

These are the feet of the One who came upon 'Legion'
and threw out the evil spirit.

These are the feet that stood firm as the paralysed – walked.

These are the feet that walked in city streets, in temples,
and were trampled upon, 'Who touched me?'

These are the feet that were immersed in the water
of a cruel northerly storm.
'Master, help us!' ... 'O ye of little faith.'

These are the feet that stood at the tomb of Lazarus
as he was bid to come out.

These are the feet on which expensive perfume was poured,
and which were caressed with the world's eternal Love.

These are the feet of the One who knelt before all humankind,
and washed their feet in humble respect for the marginalised.

These are the feet that knelt in prayer whilst others slept.

These are the feet that trod the Way in Gethsemane.

These are the feet that stood before Pilate.

These are the feet that were tortured, spat upon and beaten.

These are the feet that dragged a cross up to Calvary.

These are the feet that fell and went through unparalleled pain.
And these are the feet that were nailed to that cross
for you and me.

Pause

Listen to the silence all around you …

These are the Resurrected feet which Thomas held, and so believed.

These are the Resurrected feet that walked to Emmaus.

These are the feet
of the Resurrected Christ …
who is alive
and who will reign for all eternity.

May Christ walk with you.
And should the going get rough,
I pray He will carry you.
Amen.

Peter Phillips

The road to Emmaus (A song)

(Metre: 87 87)

Christ is risen! Greet the sunlight
streaming, still, on this great day,
burning back all mists and shadows,
lighting up our pilgrim way.

Christ is risen! He will find us
as we walk the road of care.
Still his spirit burns within us,
raises hope, dispels despair.

Christ is risen! Christ is with us,
walks beside us, unseen friend;
gives us strength to go the journey,
strong companion to its end.

Christ is risen! We shall find him
where his bread is broken, shared;
where we struggle for God's justice;
where our lives are risked and dared.

Christ is risen! All God's people
sing God's praise and live God's way,
so the church, God's love receiving,
may prepare the kingdom's day.

Stuart J Brock

Signs of hope

Introduction

'Blessed be the God and Father of our Lord Jesus Christ! By his great mercy he has given us a new birth into a living hope through the resurrection of Jesus Christ from the dead ...'

(1 Peter 1:3, NRSV)

When I began editing this book, back in winter 2020, I sent out this invitation to a wee group of Iona Community folk:

'Greetings from Wild Goose Publications. Wild Goose is publishing a book of readings for Holy Week/Easter 2021. For one part of the book, we are looking to gather some stories of HOPE from around the world.

Can you please send us a wee story about where you can see signs of hope in your part of the world, in your community, in your life? About where you can see the Kingdom breaking through ... Thank you so much for thinking about this.'

And so, here is what folk sent back, ending with a few poems I included myself, and an invitation to you, the reader, to please include your own stories and poems. Thank you.

Hope and peace,

Neil Paynter (Editor)

The New Year's light

I experience hope with the coming of the New Year's light. Winter is dark in Alaska. The Tlingits say that Raven is the Giver of light. The shortest day of the year precedes the Birth of the Christ by only a few days in December. John's Gospel says that *'In the beginning was the Word ... the Word shines in the darkness, and the darkness has not overcome it.'*

Israel Nelson, Wasilla, Alaska, New Year 2021

The hope that lies within me

As Covid struck in 2020, I found myself early in March in St Vincent's Medical Center, Bridgeport, Connecticut having double bypass surgery.

As I recovered at my daughter's house, my granddaughter Scarlett explained to the family what had happened:

'Granny died and grandpa's heart broke.'

As I peer into 2021 I know that I cannot expect the same familiar things but need to be open to new promptings of the Spirit and new and very different challenges. With Peter's encouragement in 1 Peter 3:15 I will try to give account of the hope that lies within me; a hope that has been part of my faith over the years but now takes on new shape, new direction, new surprises.

Willie Salmond, Connecticut, USA

Working for a more perfect day

June, 2020:

The murder of George Floyd was like a lightning strike on the tinder-dry ground of systemic racism in America, racism grounded in white violence against the earth, against the indigenous people of this country, against the slaves that provided the engine for the growth of a capitalist system that puts profits over the people and then securely institutionalises it by conservative judicial interpretations of our Constitution. Increasingly, a small minority, almost exclusively white, seems to be favoured instead of *'we the people'*.

However, since the murder of George Floyd, I have seen a surprisingly broad and rapid attempt on the part of white people in this country to listen, learn and act in response to our white privilege. What gives me the most hope is that young folks are out front and very determined.

Aida DeWeese-Boyd, 17, along with her brother, Jesse, 19, are members of our northern New England Iona Family Group. I do not know how intimately children in Family Groups in the UK are involved, but these two have been alongside us since the beginning of our meetings eight years ago. They were never shielded from the tough, emotional and deep discussions we have had.

Aida organised a Black Lives Matter protest in her small town in Massachusetts. They expected a couple of dozen people. A couple of hundred showed up. Her mother, Margie DeWeese-Boyd, reports: 'Aida personally invited the Georgetown police – the entire force showed up, including a few state troopers, who joined in and took a knee with the crowd for a silent 8 minutes and 46 seconds.'

These acts of solidarity and justice have been repeated in thousands of small towns across America over the past few weeks. Violence has been rare. Time and time again, the pictures show young people out front. The protests, along with countless statements of support for Black Lives Matter by large and small businesses, other non-profit groups, academia, the media, make me feel as if the people of America are beginning to hear and listen …

I am reminded to always be ready to celebrate the signs of the dawning of God's community on earth. I see that in the faces of the young, determined to work for a more perfect day. Praise be to God.

Katharine M Preston, New York State, USA, from a longer reflection

Growing hope for the future

It gives me hope to know that America's long suppressed secrets are out. When someone speaks of the riot at our Capitol on January 6, 2021, saying 'this is not who we are', today many others are quick to correct them. It *is* who we are, more truly than we want to own up to. The United States is not the country we have pretended to be. Growing numbers of us are facing we are a country founded with African slaves exploited for their labour and on land usurped via the attempted genocide of the indigenous people of the Americas. Until family histories are spoken of honestly, no true healing can begin. May this self-knowledge give us growing hope for the future.

Mark Reeve, Decatur, Georgia, USA

The Poor People's Campaign (PPC)

'The Poor People's Campaign: A National Call for Moral Revival' gives me hope. Here in the U.S., the PPC brings together people of all faiths, all races and all socio-economic backgrounds in a sustained campaign for social and economic justice. I am encouraged and empowered by its moral clarity, its ability to bring people together and its strategic vision for accomplishing the changes we so desperately need in this country:

www.poorpeoplescampaign.org

Leslie Withers, Decatur, Georgia, USA

Million Moments for Democracy

Thirty-one years ago, when the countries in the Eastern Bloc started their journey from totalitarian communist regimes towards democracy, after the collapse of the Berlin Wall, the Czech dissident and then President of the country, Václav Havel, coined the slogan *'Love and truth must prevail'*. But to these two values belongs a third one – justice. It is missing not only in the slogan; it is missing in our country. It is missing in a number of countries in the world.

For us, the hope for the Czech Republic is in the movement 'Million Moments for Democracy'. People are encouraged to think of kinds of injustice happening in the places where they live, and are asked to be active, to give their energy, time and money to ensure that love, truth and justice will prevail. The movement has spread to hundreds of places, big and also very small, throughout the Czech Republic. It is our hope that a change will happen not only in our country. We hope that love, truth and justice will spread to many places which suffer from injustice in a variety of ways.

Daniela and Tomas Bisek, Czech Republic

So many people had helped him

For the past four years I have been teaching German to refugees. One of my students was Malek, a Muslim from Syria. Shortly after he had joined the class he was diagnosed with an incurable liver disease. His only chance of survival was a transplant. When I heard this, my heart sank. He had no financial means and no health insurance. And as far as transplants are concerned, there is a list. Normally one has to wait one's turn.

The following week Malek did not show up. And nobody saw him for the next five months. Then, miraculously, the door of our classroom opened – and in came Malek, beaming with joy. He had received the transplant almost immediately – so many people had helped him to get well again. And because he was good in languages, he had a plan to study interpretation. There was hope again ...

Reinhild Traitler-Espiritu, Switzerland

Saidiana: A project of hope

Too many years ago, more than I care to remember, my husband and I visited Iona for the first time. There we met Fridah Wafula, a volunteer with the Iona Community who was putting together a business plan for a project in her home village of Matunda in Kenya. She eventually returned home with something like £800, donated by other volunteers, members of the Iona Community, guests of the Iona Centres and others to commence the work (with the help of her husband, Marksen Masinde).

This birthed the Saidiana Project – which is alive and well today. It operates to train and support women to undertake work which will provide an income so that they can feed and sustain their families. Saidiana offers training in knitting and sewing, in agricultural skills, water harvesting information, HIV/AIDS care, and business planning. It also provides micro-credit and help to people to start up small local businesses, like market stalls.

The last time I was in Kenya, I saw the new training house which was getting ready to open its doors. It is situated in a highly populated area where alcohol and drug addiction are rife. In addition to the training house, there were plans to construct some basic huts within the safety of its compound; these will act as refuges for women fleeing violence.

Saidiana also offers relief supplies in times of crisis. I visited a local family who, having taken in a child, now house around 40 youngsters who had no one to care for them, and are supported in this endeavour by the local Saidiana Project.

This project, which was conceived in Scotland and born in Kenya, desperately needs our continued support. Donations and prayers would be most welcome: please contact, *stewartandmary@gmail.com*

Madge Irving, Scotland

An encouraging story

One thing that has been continuously affirmed ever since the world plunged head first into the Covid-19 pandemic is ... *the Kingdom of God was never in crisis*. While we cannot deny the reality of jobs and incomes that were lost, businesses that closed down, families in crisis, and lives that were lost, we can also not deny the evidence of God at work in the midst of it all. From souls that came to Christ, businesses and people that thrived through the Covid-19 period, to people who received healing from the brink of death.

One encouraging story is that of a family who discovered, in March 2020, that they were 'just a bunch of strangers living under the same roof'. Over the years, work and school busyness had caused parents and children to drift apart. So they decided to be intentional about creating and cultivating family relationships. Part of the process was visiting a family therapist to help heal areas of tension. Now they have better family relations than ever. Their testimony is that Covid-19 served as a light that highlighted a problem that would have cost them their family in the future.

And for those who are yet to find anything good to say about 2020, remember that you are alive, so God's not done with you yet. Life is lived forward but understood looking back.

Fridah Wafula and Marksen Masinde, the Saidiana Project, Kenya

The Tree of Life

Iona Community member June Walker's childhood dream of going to Africa *'like a missionary but not as a missionary'* took shape in August 1957 when she arrived at Blantyre in Nyasaland. Just turned 22, recently married and with her first child on the way, she knew she was there to stay. She is.

In 1986, she and her husband, Brian, planted a *msamba mfumu*, a pod mahogany tree, by the lake in the Mangochi Peninsula, as they made a start on their retirement home. They called it the Tree of Life. It provided the shade for Brian's funeral, and Brian and June's father, Leo, are at rest in the food forest at the top of the hill. The tree is as tall and broad and strong as ever and it continues to offer shade for the permaculture classes held there. A recent permaculture permutation is *kachasu* (full-strength local brew) with lemon juice as hand sanitiser for C-19.

June Walker, Malawi

(June Walker is known as 'the mother of permaculture' in Malawi, Ed.)

Light in the darkness

A sign of hope, actually from back when we were working in Bombay, but which is timeless, and has always remained with us as a very special sign of the Kingdom breaking through – thanks to an unknown Hindu devotee:

A dark night in Mumbai – dark because a municipal strike meant that many of the streetlights were out. We walked home trying to avoid the stench of accumulating rubbish.

On a little ledge in a tree, someone had lit a tiny votive lamp – Light in darkness!

We continued our walk: our small world now transformed by that unknown Hindu person.

Frances Hawkey, England

Good news stories from around the world

See, Amnesty International Good News:

https://www.amnesty.org.uk/issues/good-news

From David Hawkey, England

Hope is leading to action

Churches working together; no-waste projects; odd veggies being delivered weekly; a recycling market where all sorts are collected, even biro pens; allotment encouragement; communities and people helping each other …

This pandemic to me has shone a light on the need for community and re-adjustment of focuses. It seems here in Brighton that more and more people are waking up to living parallel to our Iona Community Rule. There is an ever-increasing awareness of supporting each other, the environment and sustainability. HOPE is leading to ACTION. Praise God.

Jean Belgrove, England

Steve can still laugh

I volunteer weekly at a local homeless shelter. Over lockdown things have been a little different, but the shelter is still working tirelessly to help those in emergency accommodation and those yet to find a safe place off the streets.

Every time I go I find new reasons to have hope. Last week a client, Steve, arrived to hear a staff member complain about tooth pain. Without missing a beat Steve said he could offer him one of his own teeth to replace the painful one. Laughing, the staff member commented, 'At least you've got teeth. Not many people here do.' Steve nodded sincerely and laughed too. 'Yes, at least I have my own teeth.'

Even living a life of uncertainty, hunger and difficulty, Steve can still laugh and find true gratitude.

Laura Gisbourne, a member of the Iona Community Young Adults Group

Just to get a better view

It is rush hour and I am trudging home in the gathering dusk, being overtaken by a cyclist huffing his way up the steep hill. As I approach the roundabout the traffic is swarming around and the headlights are blinding in the dim grey light.

A movement catches my eye, causing me to look up: it is the cyclist from before. He is standing in the middle of the footbridge above the road, bike propped up against the railings as he uses both hands to hold his phone and take a picture. I pause, wondering what has captured his attention on this dreary weekday evening. When I glance behind me, looking down over the river I have crossed and the hill I have climbed, I know. Looking in this direction the sky is far from grey and the sinking sun is slipping below the horizon, creating a striking silhouette of the castle. I smile, and continue up the hill.

Several minutes later I am overtaken by the cyclist yet again, and this confuses me. Wasn't he heading in the other direction over the bridge? Why is he passing me once more? The only explanation I can come up with is that he went out of his way, climbing and descending all those steps with a heavy load … just to get a better view.

Laura Murray, a member of the Iona Community Young Adults Group

Something more

Light streams in through the window
bathing the room in gold,
casting out the cold.
How persistent is the dawn,
how dependable the dusk.
Like our God, steadfast and just.

Although consistent,
it's always different.
The cloud patterns change,
the colours range.
Reminding us
God has more to reveal,
our God, no box can conceal:
beauty beyond what we can describe.
Love limitless, eternal, we cannot define.

I sit and watch the sun rise and set
on days darkened by fear or regret.
There is light and hope from our divine Maker.
There is something more, Someone greater.

Rebekah Wilson, a member of the Iona Community Young Adults Group

Hope (in two poems from Iona)

No.1

Stillness
interrupted
intensified
by birdsong – solo and chorus
crashing waves
radiant sunrise
waiting
for the first snowdrop to emerge from the dark soil
when renewed hope will stir within
Keeping watch

No.2

Precarious, unsure, vulnerable
When will we know when the Abbey will reopen to guests
We're preparing
      and preparing
but the date keeps moving back
      and the doors remain closed
Still
we keep going
      tested by each other's foibles
      enriched by each other's generosity
      cherished in community
trusting the One
      in whom we have our being
      by whom we are loved
      through whom we join with our sisters and brothers
            to heed the world's cries
            to heal the world's wounds
            to hope for the world's rebirth from the coffin of Covid

and always
looking forward
to flinging wide the doors of welcome and embrace
      precarious, vulnerable
          hope-full

Caro Penney, volunteer on Iona, January 2021

At Noor

In spring 2019, I visited Palestine with a group from Derby, staying in Bethlehem in the West Bank. On a programme of visits we went to 'Aida Camp', which, after 70 years, is a small town housing over six thousand internally displaced Palestinians ...

At Noor
we drank dark welcoming coffee from tiny paper cups,
then Islam, mother of six children, and her friend
helped us prepare *maqluba* for our lunch,
chopping eggplant, shiny peppers, onions,
mixing spices, fresh herbs and laughter
together round the table at Aida Camp.

And whilst the meal was cooking we went to see the sights –
escorted by our guide, who knows no other place –
the grey and narrow streets, the broken paving,
grim dividing WALL, graffiti displaying sadness, patience,
anger – and some humour. Stark barrier
imprisoning its people.

Then food, offered with smiles, with graciousness
at Noor – the Arabic for hope –
accompanied with sweet *basbousa* cake
in Bethlehem.

Jill Rhodes

Birds over Nablus (2013)

A day spent in the company
of two young men
both sons of this
ancient city
who shared
heartbreaking stories
of freedom curtailed or
brutally denied.
Later, drinking tea
in the hotel,
I saw through an
open window,
hundreds of birds,
circling above
the skyline;
summoned by some
deep instinct.
Gathering, preparing
to migrate;
free to cross borders,
ignore checkpoints,
surveillance cameras –
free to fly!
As darkness fell,
came the haunting
call to prayer
from a nearby mosque
summoning humans
un-free, yet born to rise.

Warren R Bardsley

RSVP to a chain letter

An e-mail invitation to share a poem with 22 other random people was circulating during the lockdown in 2020.

Thank you for inviting me
to join you in flying a kite,
but I fear this one won't fly:
the synthetic string's far too tangled
and I don't know where it begins or ends.

> Instead, look up:
> the sky is full now
> of homemade kites created with love,
> launched by those
> who are earthbound and lonely.

I choose to join
the spontaneity of this dance.

Jan Sutch Pickard, March 2020

I have a voice

Through my life I've had many downs as well as some ups. Having the support that people give me has helped me tremendously. Through coaching and support you can achieve most things in life, like writing poems. Having support means a great deal to people that don't believe in themselves.

i am hidden small and dainty
issues with health and motivation
my world is crumbling around me
my pain is hidden from all to see

i have a voice

abused and berated downcast
shunned by government and society
unloved and forgotten

i have a voice

i use my voice
loud and clear
shout and scream
for all to hear
more articulate
more knowledge
and more motivation

i am here to help to use my voice
to speak up for those who can't
who are hidden like me
who feel that there is no hope
i have a voice

Penny Walters, Church Action on Poverty

Signs of hope (to the reader)

Where do you see signs of hope? Where can you see the Kingdom breaking through? ...

BLESSING

Scattered in so many places

God in community,
who scatters yourself in creating, redeeming and sustaining,
hear our prayers for the work of our community:

into the silence surrounding oppression,
may we be a strong voice;

into the shadows of despair,
may we be the light of hope;

into the brokenness of lives,
may we be healing and strength;

into the emptiness of loneliness,
may we be a friend and family;

into the absence of faith,
may we be your face and heart.

Thom M Shuman

About the Contributors

Warren R Bardsley is a retired minister living in Lichfield; has served as a human rights observer in Jerusalem and the West Bank with the WCC Ecumenical Accompaniment Programme, and has written three books on the Palestinian struggle for justice and human rights. He is one of the founder members of the Kairos Britain movement.

Jean Belgrove is a member of the Iona Community.

Daniela and Tomas Bisek became associate members of the Iona Community in the early 1990s, when they lived in Scotland after having been made to emigrate from Czechoslovakia by the communist authorities because they had signed Charter 77.

Stuart J Brock: Ordained into ministry of the United Reformed Church in 1975 after training in Cambridge. Served in Manchester and Tyneside until early retirement on health grounds in 2004. Since then has spent time in creative writing and music, as well as enjoying the open air, walking in the countryside of Northumberland and Durham. Draws inspiration from the story of Christianity in NE England. Has written a number of hymns, one or two of which have been published.

Ruth Burgess is a member of the Iona Community who lives in Dunblane. She enjoys being retired, writing and editing, growing fruit, flowers and vegetables, and paddling along the seashore whenever possible.

Church Action on Poverty is a national ecumenical Christian social justice charity, committed to tackling poverty in the UK.

> We work in partnership with churches, and with people in poverty themselves, to tackle the root causes of poverty.
>
> We put gospel values of justice and compassion into practice.
>
> We know that the real experts on poverty are the people who live with it. Our work is driven by their insights and experiences.
>
> We help them to make their voices heard. We speak truth to power, campaigning nationally and locally for policies that will loosen the grip of poverty on people's lives.
>
> *(From the Church Action on Poverty website: www.church-poverty.org.uk)*

Nancy Cocks is a retired minister and former Deputy Warden on Iona, who continues to develop liturgical resources and works in refugee resettlement in Medicine Hat, Alberta, Canada.

The Corrymeela Community: In our increasingly divided world, Corrymeela is a movement of people rallied around one inspirational idea: 'Together is better'.

> Every year we welcome over 8,000 people, from all walks of life, to our beautiful Ballycastle home and into our programmes in communities around Northern Ireland.
>
> We deeply believe that everyone is welcome, whatever their background, ethnicity, faith, sexuality or nationality.
>
> We welcome everyone – because together is better.
>
> From programmes enabling young people to tackle sectarianism, to supporting survivors of racism and homophobia, we work relentlessly to tackle intolerance, hatred and oppression.
>
> We challenge injustice – because together is better.
>
> As we hear each other's story, we learn how to live well with each other.
>
> We change ourselves – because together is better.
>
> And, we'd love to welcome you.
>
> Because together is better.
>
> *(From the Corrymeela Community website: www.corrymeela.org)*

Murphy Davis had a big heart and wide-reaching arms that embraced a huge circle of friends. Among those who benefited from her loving care and relentless advocacy were prisoners on Georgia's death row and people living on the streets, whom she served for more than four decades. Murphy was a Presbyterian pastor who spent her life in the struggle for civil and human rights. She and her husband, Ed Loring, founded the Open Door Community in downtown Atlanta. Murphy wrote *Surely Goodness and Mercy*, a memoir of her 25-year journey with cancer, which was published shortly before her passing in October 2020. The ache of her absence is still raw for the many friends who have loved her over the years. To order a copy of *Surely Goodness and Mercy*, e-mail David Payne at davidpayne@opendoorcommunity.org

Judy Dinnen: Anglican minister and Iona associate, who enjoys a variety of creative challenges. These include poetry, readings and workshops.

About the contributors

Carol Dixon is a lay preacher in the United Reformed Church. She writes regularly for godspacelight.com, her hymns can be found on HymnQuest, in *Church Hymnary 4*, and a CD of her Holy Island hymns was produced for St Cuthbert's, Holy Island. She is a wife, mother and grandmother and enjoys going for walks with her seven grandchildren.

Brian Ford: 'I am a retired biology teacher, at present studying for an M.A. in Theology. I'm an amateur gardener, poet, folk singer and actor.'

Craig Gardiner grew up in the North of Ireland and is married to Meredith from Scotland. They met on a Wild Goose Worship Week on Iona! Together, they live in Wales with their two children Niamh (13) and Euan (10) and a Labrador puppy called Amber. This mix of family nations generally works well (apart from occasions of international rugby fixtures). Craig is a Baptist minister and works as a theology tutor in Cardiff University and South Wales Baptist College. He is the author of a recent book on Iona and Bonhoeffer, *Melodies of a New Monasticism: Bonhoeffer's Vision, Iona's Witness*, SCM, 2018.

Laura Gisbourne is a member of the Iona Community Young Adults Group and is using her time during furlough to volunteer at a local homeless shelter.

Tom Gordon is a retired Church of Scotland minister, and former hospice chaplain and bereavement care facilitator. Now resident East Lothian, he writes extensively: www.ionabooks.com, https://swallowsnestnet.wordpress.com

Ruth Harvey lives in Cumbria, where she enjoys upside-down views of lakes and fells. She worships with the Quakers, has been a member of the Iona Community since 1993, and Leader since June 2020.

David Hawkey: 'I was blessed by a privileged education, leading to teaching in city schools and museums. With Frances, the vision broadened as an exciting journey in ecumenism, interfaith and engaged spirituality through Taizé and the Iona Community, and exploring where God was to be found on Greenham Common (with CND), in Bombay, on a Tottenham estate and in Coventry through the Cathedral's Cross of Nails.'

Frances Hawkey: 'I am an associate member of the Iona Community and worked as Abbey Housekeeper for a year. With David, my husband, I lived in Bombay (Mumbai) for ten years, and on a London Council estate for another ten. Deep friendships with people of different faiths and cultures have enlarged my own faith and being more than I can measure.'

Madge Irving: 'My late husband and I made the connection with Fridah from Saidiana when she was a volunteer on Iona. When we visited her and Marksen in Kenya, we were warmly welcomed, and their friendship has greatly widened our understanding of the various cultures in our world. Their faith and mentoring has also fostered in me a love for Africa and, in addition to my support for Saidiana, I have been a trustee for a charity in Malawi for the past 10 years.'

Martin Johnstone works alongside a range of social justice organisations with a particular commitment to ensuring that the wisdom of people struggling against poverty is heard and acted upon. You can find out more about what he is up to at *www.attheedge.co.uk*. He is an associate member of the Iona Community.

Fiona Kendall is European and Legal Affairs Advisor of Mediterranean Hope (*www.mediterraneanhope.com*). She is an associate member of the Iona Community.

Janet Killeen studied English and American literature, and taught in a London comprehensive school for over thirty-five years. She has published poems, short stories and two novels, and is the author of *Towards Bethlehem: Stories & Poems for Advent, Christmas & Epiphany*, Wild Goose Publications, 2020

Charlotte Killeya: 'I rediscovered my love of writing a few years ago when I joined the creative writing group at Parson Cross Initiative (PXI) in Sheffield. I had always enjoyed writing, but over the years I lost inspiration and confidence. The group really helped and supported me. I enjoy writing about the things I observe and the people who I meet in my everyday life. I am also a volunteer and trustee for PXI.'

S Anne Lawson is Vicar of the Cross Country Parishes of Acton, Church Minshull, Worleston and Wettenhall, and Chaplain to the Cheshire Agricultural Society. She shares her home with her two cats. Writing poetry is a way of working out theology, and holding paradoxes in tension.

Janet Lees is a writer who uses a remembered Bible. A former School Chaplain, she is a member of the Lay Community of St Benedict. She has two books and several downloads published by Wild Goose and is a regular contributor to their anthologies. You can read her blog at https://foowr.org.uk/notesfrombambi/ and follow her on Twitter @Bambigoesforth.

Emma Major is a pioneer lay minister, blind wheelchair user and poet. She has written a number of books, including being the author and illustrator of *Little*

Guy: Journey of Hope, Wild Goose Publications. You can find her blogging at http://LLMCalling.blogspot.com

Marksen Masinde is a friend of the Iona Community, and with Fridah Wafula works for Saidiana in Kenya.

John McCall has lived and served in Taiwan for over twenty years. He accompanies seminary students, Asian pastors and the indigenous people of Taiwan. He is an associate of the Iona Community.

Peter Millar is a theologian, campaigner and writer who has worked in many parts of the world, including Iona as Abbey Warden. For the last five years he has lived with an incurable cancer. He is a soul friend to many.

Laura Murray is a member of the Iona Community Young Adults Group, from Glasgow, but currently studying at the University of Edinburgh (MSc Medical Anthropology).

Israel Nelson is enjoying retirement from ministry and work as a substance abuse treatment professional. He lives in Alaska, where he watches Mother Moose teach her babies how to enjoy God's creation.

The Open Door Community is a residential community in the Catholic Worker tradition (we're sometimes called a Protestant Catholic Worker House). We seek to dismantle racism, sexism and hetero-sexism, abolish the death penalty, and proclaim the Beloved Community through loving relationships with some of the most neglected and outcast of God's children: the homeless and our sisters and brothers who are in prison. *(From the Open Door website: https://opendoorcommunity.org)*

Neil Paynter is an editor, writer and late-night piano player, who previously worked in homeless shelters and nursing homes. He lives in a flat in Biggar, Scotland with his partner Helen, his mum and Stevie the cat.

Caro Penney has, over the last few years, been letting life evolve beyond its previous expectations and is currently, for the first time, living in community and wearing the Housekeeper's apron at Iona Abbey! On 29 May this year, she will be celebrating 50 years since her very first visit to the Abbey Church – and reflecting on the journey since then with the Iona Community, including as a member.

Peter Phillips lives in the Cathedral City of Lichfield in the English Midlands. He began writing poetry after he had been diagnosed with motor neuron disease. His poetry has brought comfort and reassurance to many.

Jan Sutch Pickard is a poet and storyteller living on Mull. After six years on the staff of the Iona Community, latterly as Warden of the Abbey, she volunteered with the Ecumenical Accompaniment Programme in Palestine and Israel, serving for two tours of duty – only six months altogether, but a profound and life-changing experience – like Iona.

Chris Polhill is the Iona Community's Prayer Circle Coordinator. She is the author of several Wild Goose books, including *A Heart for Creation: Worship Resources and Reflections on the Environment*.

Katharine M Preston is an ecumenical lay preacher and writer, concentrating on issues of social justice and climate change. She is the author of *Field with a View: Science and Faith in a Time of Climate Change*, Wild Goose Publications, 2019, and is active in the Community's Common Concern Network focusing on the environment. Katharine and her husband, John Bingham, live on a farm in Essex, New York and are active associates of the Iona Community.

Mark Reeve became aware of social justice issues in the era of the Vietnam War. He and his partner, Leslie Withers, are active members of Oakhurst Baptist Church in Decatur, Georgia, USA and have been associates of the Iona Community since 2012.

Jill Rhodes: 'I am an Iona associate and retired counsellor living in Wirksworth, Derbyshire.'

Willie Salmond is a retired minister of the Presbyterian Church of Ghana. He lives in Westport, Connecticut and often travels back to Uganda, where he was Regional Director of Africa Management for the Elizabeth Glaser Pediatric AIDS Foundation, to renew his understanding of scripture. His new novel, *Deep Secrets* – about terror and romance in the heart of Africa – is available from Waterstones.

Rev'd Sr Sandra Sears, CSBC is a Local Priest in the Anglican Diocese of Willochra in South Australia. She is also a sister in the Community of Sts Barnabas and Cecilia. A well as writing poetry, stories and liturgies, she composes songs and hymns, some of which have been published in hymnals.

Thom M Shuman is a retired, yet still active, pastor. He is the author of several books, including *How Shall We Pray This Morning? For What Shall We Pray This Night?: A Month of Worship Resources for a Time of Pandemic* (Wild Goose). He is an associate of the Iona Community.

Matt Sowerby is a spoken word poet and activist from Cumbria. He has performed in the Houses of Parliament, at TEDxDoncaster and at The Poetry Society. In 2018 he became a National Youth Poetry Slam Champion. In 2019 his poem-play *Kids These Days* premiered at Greenbelt Festival. Matt is currently studying at the University of Birmingham and is co-founder of the community activist group KASTLE. Throughout lockdown, Matt has been the Poet In Digital Residence at Church Action on Poverty. During this time, he ran a series of workshops and open mics, as well as coordinating the creation of *Same Boat: Poems on Poverty and Lockdown*.

Reinhild Traitler-Espiritu: former Director of the Boldern Protestant Academy, Zurich, member of the Interreligious ThinkTank, Switzerland, and co-founder of the European Project for Interreligious Learning (EPIL).

Fridah Wafula is an associate member of the Iona Community, and the Founder of Saidiana in Kenya.

June Walker (née Bottrill) was not born with green fingers. In her probationary year as a teacher at Broughton High School, Salford, 1956-1957, none of the pupils in her class of 30 was successful in growing beans. Then she married Brian Walker, who was born with green fingers and had hoped to be a farmer. In the 1980s, in Malawi, they heard about a rocky plot of land by the lake where no one grew food. This coincided with learning about permaculture from Jeremy Burnham, who was based in South Africa. The message was about how to grow food without using chemicals or financial input. There are three basic principles: care for the earth, care for people and share the surplus. That is all it is. It is localised and people teach it wherever they are.

Penny Walters: 'I have worked alongside Church Action on Poverty, Sustain and Food Nation on the Food Power programme for over three years. During this time I have used my own lived experience to campaign both locally and nationally on food poverty issues. I've co-designed participation tools as part of the Leapfrog Project with Lancaster University, attended the 'Closing the Hunger Gap' conference in North Carolina and spoken to MPs, alongside local and national media. Since Covid-19 I've given evidence to the House of Lords Select Committee on Food, Poverty, Health and the Environment, whilst also becoming involved in online creative workshops, giving me another way to express my feelings during lockdown. I'll continue the fight against poverty both in Byker and across the UK.'

Rebekah Wilson is a medical student living and studying in Glasgow. She is continually discovering more of who God is and has various wonderful friends who challenge her and teach her a lot. In her free time, she loves to cook, run, swim and write poetry.

Leslie Withers is a member of Oakhurst Baptist Church in Decatur, Georgia, USA, and is on the Georgia State Coordinating Council for the 'Poor People's Campaign: A National Call for Moral Revival'. She and her husband, Mark Reeve, are associate members of the Iona Community.

Brian Woodcock is a retired URC minister, a member of the Iona Community and a former Iona Abbey Warden. He retired to Bristol with his wife, Sheila, fourteen and a half years ago.

Martin Wroe is a writer, occasional broadcaster and volunteer vicar in Holloway, north London. Among his spiritual guides in recent times are Meg Wroe, Mavis Staples, the Iona Community, Laura Marling, Arsène Wenger, Neil Astley, Kae Tempest and Michael Kiwanuka.

SOURCES AND ACKNOWLEDGEMENTS

Passages from NRSV copyright 1989, Division of Christian Education of the National Council of the Churches of Christ in the United States of America. Used by permission. All rights reserved.

Some of Tom Gordon's pieces in this book are from his online daily blog: 'Tom Gordon, Hymns and Reflections': https://swallowsnestnet.wordpress.com

'Children of the stones', by Warren R Bardsley, from *Occasional Poems*, Warren R Bardsley, Church in the Market Place Publications, 2020. To order this book, please contact: w.bardsley39@btinternet.com

Prayers from the Corrymeela Community from *Prayers for Community in a Time of Pandemic* © the Corrymeela Community, www.corrymeela.org. Used by permission of the Corrymeela Community.

'Who touched me?', by Peter Phillips, from *e-Coracle*, the online magazine of the Iona Community, 2020, Neil Paynter (Ed.)

'In these strange times', from *e-Coracle*, the online magazine of the Iona Community, 2020, Neil Paynter (Ed.)

'The source of happiness', by Murphy Davis, from *A Work of Hospitality: The Open Door Reader: 1982–2002*, Peter R Gathje (Ed), the Open Door Community, 2002, pp.227-229. Used by permission of Ed Loring.

'Mediterranean Hope', by Fiona Kendall, from *e-Coracle*, the online magazine of the Iona Community, 2020, Neil Paynter (Ed.)

'Remembering', by Peter Millar, from *A Time to Mend: Reflections in Uncertain Times*, Wild Goose Publications, 2013. Used by permission of Peter Millar.

'Breathe 2' © Matt Sowerby, from *Same Boat: Poems on Poverty and Lockdown*, Church Action on Poverty, 2020. Used by permission of Matt Sowerby and CAP. *Same Boat* 'brings together dozens of works by people with experience of poverty and supporters from across the movement to end poverty': https://www.church-poverty.org.uk/sameboatpoems/

'Cross in the bus station', by Warren R Bardsley, from *Occasional Poems*, Warren R Bardsley, Church in the Market Place Publications, 2020. To order this book, please contact: w.bardsley39@btinternet.com

'Suggestions for reflection and action on Holy Saturday', by Ruth Burgess, from *Iona Dawn: Through Holy Week with the Iona Community*, Neil Paynter (Ed.), Wild Goose Publications, 2006

'Dear diary' © Charlotte Killeya, from *Same Boat: Poems on Poverty and Lockdown*, Church Action on Poverty, 2020. Used by permission of Charlotte Killeya and CAP. *Same Boat* 'brings together dozens of works by people with experience of poverty and supporters from across the movement to end poverty': https://www.church-poverty.org.uk/sameboatpoems/

'Working for a more perfect day', by Katharine M Preston, from a longer reflection in *e-Coracle*, the online magazine of the Iona Community, 2020, Neil Paynter (Ed.)

'Saidiana: A project of hope', by Madge Irving, from a longer piece in *e-Coracle*, the online magazine of the Iona Community, 2020, Neil Paynter (Ed.)

'At Noor', by Jill Rhodes, from *e-Coracle*, the online magazine of the Iona Community, 2020, Neil Paynter (Ed.)

'Birds over Nablus (2013)', by Warren R Bardsley, from *Occasional Poems*, Warren R Bardsley, Church in the Market Place Publications, 2020. To order this book, please contact: w.bardsley39@btinternet.com

'RSVP to a chain letter', by Jan Sutch Pickard, from *Edges: Ross of Mull Poets*, Hybrid Press, 2020: https://hybriddreich.co.uk/edges-ross-of-mull-poets

'I have a voice' © Penny Walters, from *Same Boat: Poems on Poverty and Lockdown*, Church Action on Poverty, 2020. Used by permission of Penny Walters and CAP. *Same Boat* 'brings together dozens of works by people with experience of poverty and supporters from across the movement to end poverty': https://www.church-poverty.org.uk/sameboatpoems/

'Scattered in so many places', by Thom M Shuman, from *In the Gift of This New Day: Praying with the Iona Community*, Neil Paynter (Ed.), Wild Goose Publications, 2015

Wild Goose Publications, the publishing house of the Iona Community established in the Celtic Christian tradition of Saint Columba, produces books, e-books, CDs and digital downloads on:

- holistic spirituality
- social justice
- political and peace issues
- healing
- innovative approaches to worship
- song in worship, including the work of the Wild Goose Resource Group
- material for meditation and reflection

For more information:

Wild Goose Publications
The Iona Community
Suite 9, Fairfield, 1048 Govan Road
Glasgow G51 4XS, Scotland

Tel. +44 (0)141 429 7281
e-mail: admin@ionabooks.com

or visit our website at
www.ionabooks.com
for details of all our products and online sales